Liberty *for* All

This book is dedicated to the loving memory of Dr. William Kaplan—the greatest father a person could ever want. From the beginning, he was thrilled by the Statue project and my involvement in photographing this historic undertaking. Like his son, he felt great passion for the Lady in the Harbor. But for him, it was a simple love affair: She represented the country that he held close to his heart—America. For his encouragement and support, and most important of all, his love, I am forever grateful. To my mother Lillian, a gifted sculptor from whom I inherited an artist's eye that enabled me to see the Statue in a special way through the lens of a camera. And to Ed Dooley, my boss at the Statue of Liberty-Ellis Island Foundation. An advertising man from the old school, he fought to get me access to the Statue so I could take those pictures and put, as he said, a "human" face on a lifeless monument.

Last but not least to my wife Sharon and my children Ricki Liberty and Gabriel Liberty, who have always had to share their time and their home with the "special Lady". Their patience is unwavering; their love, boundless; and their sense of humor, unending. I recently heard my seven-year-old explain to a friend why our house is filled with Liberty stuff—"Because my Daddy has the Statue in his brain!"

Photographs by Peter B. Kaplan

Text by Lee Iacocca

Liberty *for* All

Edited by Barbara Grazzini

Miller Publishing, Inc.
Wilmington, Delaware

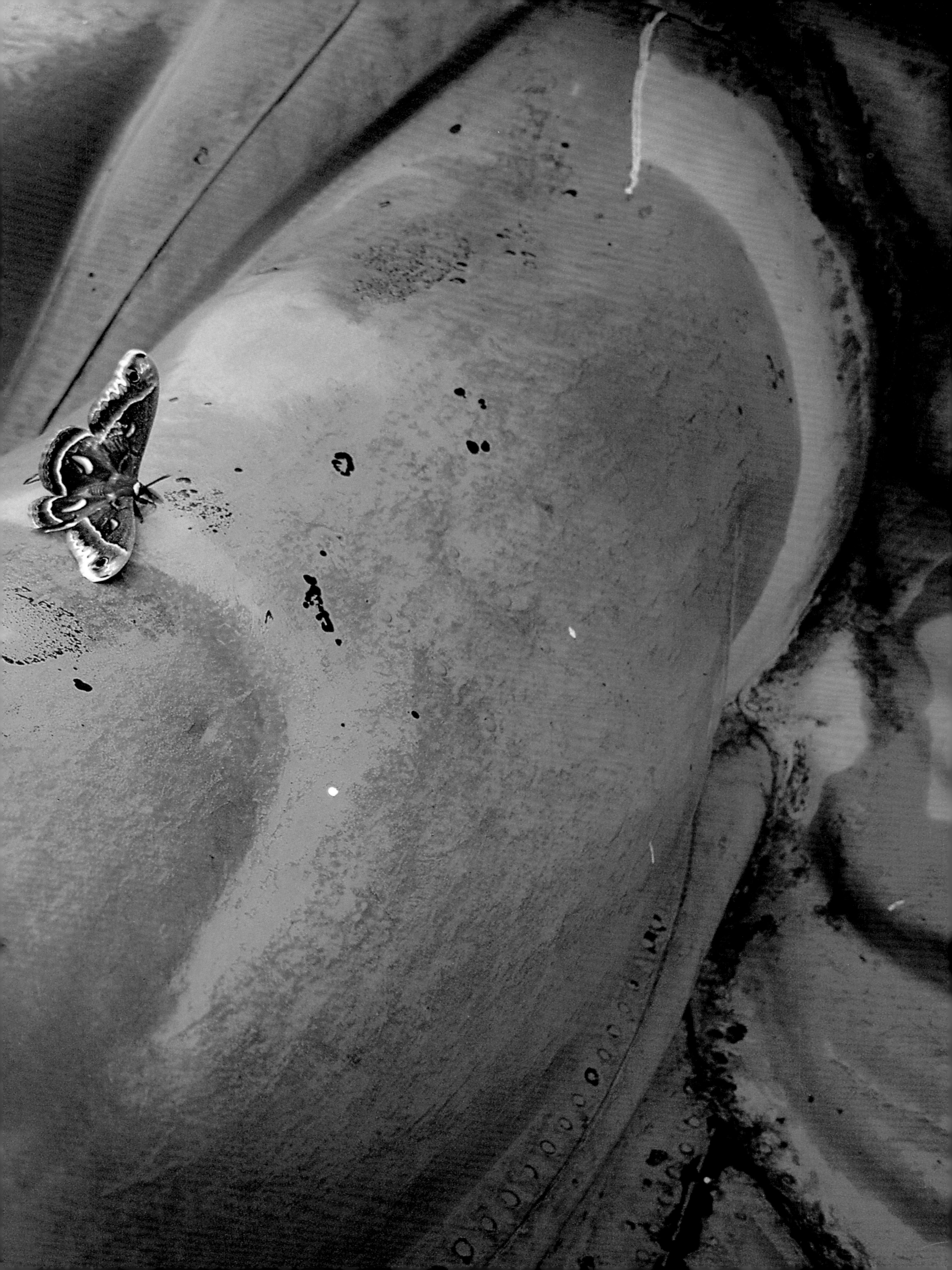

The New Colossus

Not like the brazen giant of Greek fame,
With conquering limbs astride from land to land,
Here at our sea-washed, sunset-gates shall stand
A mighty woman with a torch, whose flame
Is the imprisoned lightning, and her name
Mother of Exiles. From her beacon-hand
Glows world-wide welcome, her mild eyes command
The air-bridged harbor that twin-cities frame.

Keep, ancient lands, your storied pomp!" cries she,
With silent lips. "Give me your tired, your poor,
Your huddled masses yearning to breathe free,
The wretched refuse of your teeming shore;
Send these, the homeless, tempest-tost to me,
I lift my lamp beside the golden door!"

Emma Lazarus

Contents

Published in 2002
Printed in Korea

Library of Congress Control Number:
00-134307
ISBN: 0-9663337-1-3
First Edition October 2002

Photography Peter B. Kaplan
Text Lee Iacocca
Editor Barbara Grazzini
Design Phillip Unetic

Miller Publishing, Inc.
Frederick Miller
1201 N. Orange Street
Suite 200
Wilmington, DE 19801
www.millerpublishinginc.com
fmiller2@dscc.com

PAGE 1 *"Starburst" Fireworks celebrate the Statue of Liberty centennial in 1986.*
TITLE PAGE *Manhattan's famous skyline, perfect backdrop for the monument.*
PAGE 4-5 *"A Pole Shot" View from the torch, photographed with a remote-controlled camera mounted on a 23-foot pole.*
PAGE 6-7 *"Moth Not a Butterfly" A silkworm moth gently alights on the Statue's foot.*
PAGE 8-9 *"A Pole Shot" Liberty's beacon, lighting the way for immigrants since 1886.*
OPPOSITE *At dusk, schoolchildren gather at the Statue, symbol of America and freedom around the world.*
RIGHT *The torch afire with sunlight.*

Introduction

When I was six, my father piled the family into his beat-up old Ford and drove us from our home in Allentown, Pennsylvania all the way to New York. He wanted us to see the Statue of Liberty. We went again when I was eleven. Both times, he made my sister and me climb the 354 stairs to the crown, and along the way he talked about what the Statue represented. Looking back, I remember being awe-struck at the view from the top and not much else. She may have meant a lot to him, but frankly it was lost on us kids.

It was not until years later that I fully understood what my father was trying to say. In 1982, President Ronald Reagan asked me to lead the effort to restore the Statue of Liberty and its companion monument, Ellis Island. To pay for the projects, we solicited money from the public. With a final goal of $87 million just to overhaul the Statue, the response was overwhelming.

Young, old, rich, poor—people everywhere gave to the project. And not only did they send money, they also wrote letters—each one more moving than the next. Reading these notes, I began to understand why my father had such a special

OPPOSITE *Forever linked: The Statue of Liberty and nearby Ellis Island—gateway to America for seventeen million immigrants between 1892 and 1924.*

gleam in his eye for the Lady. For him, and the millions of immigrants who landed at nearby Ellis Island, she was a symbol of hope. And to the hundred million of us who are these immigrants' children and grandchildren, she had become a symbol of the sacrifices they made so that we could grow up free to live the American dream.

It was at the beginning of the Statue project that I ran into another immigrant descendant who was also living the American dream—photographer Peter B. Kaplan. Like me, he had a father who loved the Statue and all it represented. It was this inherited passion that drove him to begin a photographic record of the most successful public-private partnership in the history of the country.

Kaplan was there from the start. I first met him at a topping off ceremony for the scaffolding. As Peter climbed onto a precarious perch to get a better angle, Walter Cronkite, who was with me at the time, turned and asked "Is he Nuts?"—a question many would raise over the course of the next few years. Nights, days, weekends, in all kinds of weather, Peter and his camera scaled new heights to faithfully record the restoration that would captivate the nation. Now preserved in the pages of this book, his photographs put a human face on the Statue, as the giant copper monument became "she" not "it" to millions of people around the globe.

When I was first approached several years ago to write a few words for *Liberty for All*, the world was a far different place than when we celebrated the Statue's 100th birthday in 1986. Since then, old enemies of the United States have become newfound partners, as modern technology and the internet made us all global citizens. Then came September 11, 2001, and America was forever changed.

A number of the pictures in the book show the Statue set against the once familiar backdrop of the World Trade Center. Our first instinct was to replace the photos. But if we did that, we would erase all memory of what we, as Americans, should never forget. So as you thumb through these pages, know that although the Twin Towers are lost forever, the ideal that the Statue represents—freedom—remains strong in the hearts of us all.

Standing guard at the entrance to New York Harbor.

Chapter 1

History

I'm a lucky guy. I've had terrific parents, a wonderful wife, two great kids, and a career in an industry I loved. So when President Ronald Reagan asked me to head a citizen's commission to advise the government on restoring the Statue of Liberty and Ellis Island, I couldn't refuse.

My family and friends thought I was crazy to take on such a huge task. Chrysler was starting to rebound, and I had plenty of work to do in Detroit. But it was payback time, a way to say thanks to both my parents and America for opportunities that others only dream about. Besides, several years earlier the government had helped keep Chrysler afloat with a 1.5 billion dollar loan guarantee. I was hardly in a position to say no.

Washington just loves to come up with blue-ribbon commissions and ours was no different. Part political, part practical, it included people from all walks of life.

Our main goal was to consult with the Interior Department on restoring and preserving the Statue and Ellis Island. There was only one problem. While the

PRECEDING PAGES *The once familiar view of the Statue with the World Trade Center in the background, now but a memory etched forever in the hearts of all Americans.* **OPPOSITE** *Dedication of the Statue on October 28, 1886, as depicted in this Thomas Moran painting.*

panel was long on prominent names, it was short on cash. Not only did the government want us to advise on the restoration, but they also wanted us to figure out how to pay for it.

At first we projected that the Statue alone would cost $30 million to fix up, not to mention a couple of hundred million for Ellis Island. Boy, were we surprised. Like people who set out to renovate an old house, we soon learned that it would take several times that amount to do the job. And while the President, with all his good intentions, was touting volunteerism, I was pretty sure no construction firm was ever going to work for free.

With not so much as a dime in the kitty, the commission set up shop. I soon discovered another thing about government panels. They really can't do much of anything—but give advice! They can't solicit money, sign contracts, negotiate, or do a hundred other practical tasks that needed to be done to meet a deadline—the summer of '86. That's when we would throw the Lady a hundredth birthday party.

To remedy the situation, a separate organization—the non-profit Statue of Liberty-Ellis Island Foundation—was set up. The Foundation signed an agreement with the Interior Department that authorized the group to raise money. A glutton for punishment, I also became chairman of the Foundation. It meant twice as much work, but by then, restoring the two monuments was becoming a labor of love for me. Besides, I wasn't going to let people use my name to solicit donations and then not have a say in how the money was spent. I was a firm believer in accountability—all too rare a commodity nowadays in both the public and the private sectors.

The Foundation took on the added responsibility of contracting for the work and managing the construction. This meant we could cut through a lot of bureaucratic red tape, eliminate delays, and get the job done on time—seldom heard of in the federal government.

When we started, all we had was some donated office space, a handful of volunteers and a few people I enticed from the private sector. I convinced Paul Bergmoser, former president of Chrysler, to help us get started. He saw us through our first few months, and helped me convince John Morrissey, who ran Chrysler's ad

RIGHT *In 1982, President Ronald Reagan appoints Lee Iacocca, chairman of the Chrysler Corporation, to spearhead a private sector campaign to restore the Statue. A gift of the French people to America in 1886, the monument was built with money donated by ordinary French citizens to commemorate the alliance between the two nations.*

Photo: Courtesy of the Ronald Reagan Library

UNION FRANCO-AMÉRICAINE

DISCOURS

DE

MM. HENRI MARTIN, E.-B. WASHBURNE, ÉDOUARD LABOULAYE

ET J.-W. FORNEY

PRONONCÉS AU

BANQUET DU 6 NOVEMBRE 1875

AU SIEGE DU COMITÉ

175 — RUE SAINT-HONORÉ — 175

ET A LA BIBLIOTHÈQUE CHARPENTIER

13, RUE DE GRENELLE-SAINT-GERMAIN, 13

PARIS

Prix : 1 fr. 50

FAR LEFT *Souvenir from the French fundraising campaign: A program from the inaugural event in 1875.* **LEFT** *An 1886 plaque honoring the French and American alliance.*

Designing the form of Liberty

The idea of a memorial to Franco-American friendship was first proposed at a dinner in 1865 by a group of Frenchmen who admired the American ideal of liberty. In attendance was Frédéric-Auguste Bartholdi, above, a young Alsatian artist who had developed a special interest in colossal sculpture. Inspired by the idea put forth that evening, Bartholdi began designing a grandiose monument as a tribute to the deep abiding relationship between the two countries. In 1871, he journeyed to the United States to arouse interest in the project and while there, chose a small island in Upper New York Bay as the site for his work. When he returned home, he began to crystallize the shape the monument would take: a giant statue of a woman dressed in classical Greek clothes. For several years Bartholdi refined his design, but it was not until 1875 that actual construction on the monument began.

Models and an 1869 sketch for a proposed lighthouse at the Suez Canal. Bartholdi later insisted that Liberty's design had no connection with these earlier renderings.

Courtesy Musée de Bartholdi / Colmar, France

agency back in Detroit to lend a hand with our advertising. Later Bill May, a former dean at New York University, and past chairman of American Can, volunteered to come on board as CEO.

We also lucked out by hiring a young Italian, Steve Briganti, as Vice President. Steve had been an executive with the Tri-State United Way and knew the ins and outs of fundraising. He was also tight with a buck—a real plus, I learned, when you're spending other people's money.

Our game plan was to raise as much as we could from individuals. But we also knew that you don't collect millions just by passing the hat. Since I'm a corporate guy, I twisted the arm of every CEO I knew—and a few I didn't—to make a donation. By early 1983 we had raised enough funds in cash or pledges that we could start hiring people. Together with the Park Service, which ran the Statue, we rounded up some of the best architects and engineers to draw up plans.

continued on page 43

Architects and engineers from the private sector and the National Park Service review plans for restoring the monument. Begun in 1983, the overhaul took almost three years, at a cost of eighty-seven million dollars.

Bartholdi's Mother as Model

According to some historians, Bartholdi's close emotional attachment to his mother, Charlotte Bartholdi, inspired the use of her stern face as a model for that of "Liberty". Mme. Bartholdi's strong facial features—her nose, eyes, mouth, and jaw—as seen in the photograph above, and marble bust at right, are reflected in the Statue's countenance on the opposite page. A formidable woman, Mme. Bartholdi dominated her son throughout her life

PRECEDING PAGES *The artist poses in his studio in Paris, France. At the center of the photo is a model of the Statue. To the far left, a testimonial torch presented by* The World *newspaper to Bartholdi in appreciation of his work on the Statue. Tiffany's created the tribute.*

Courtesy Musée de Bartholdi / Colmar, France

In the Paris foundry of Gaget, Gauthier et Companie, workers construct Liberty's hand while the sculptor and a top-hatted visitor watch. A full-scale plaster sleeve encases the wooden skeleton. Carpenters later fabricated wooden duplicates of the plaster sections to reverse and use as molds for the Statue's copper "skin".

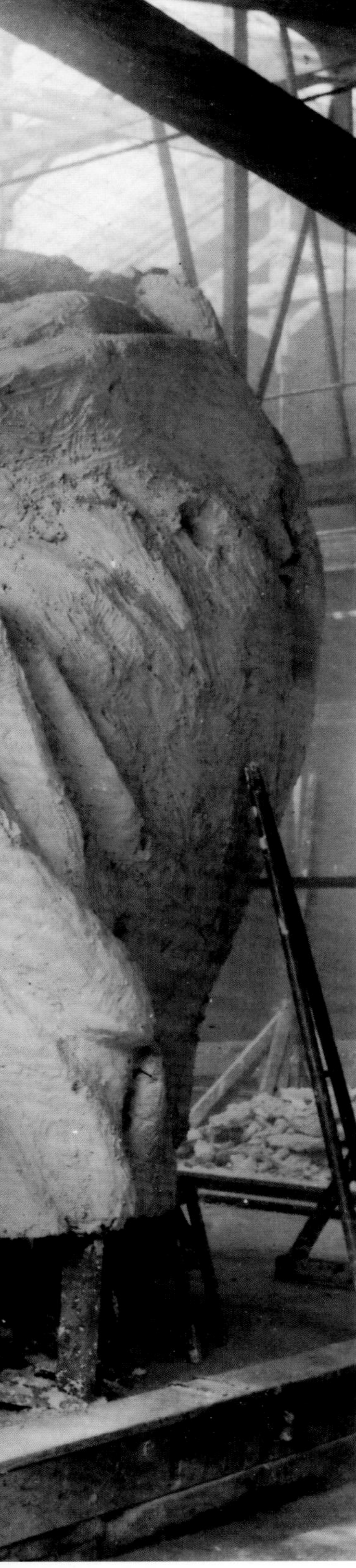

BELOW *A six inch miniature of the Statue bearing its original name, "Liberty Enlightening the World".* **RIGHT** *A souvenir silk ribbon from the 1878 Paris exhibition. To stir interest in the project, Bartholdi unveiled the Statue's completed head at the expo.*

Liberty's copper torch on display at the 1876 Centennial Exhibit in Philadelphia. Visitors paid a modest fee to climb to the top, with the money going toward paying for the Statue's pedestal.

ART DECORATIONS 13

Statue of "Liberty Enlightening the World."

The Committee in charge of the construction of the base and pedestal for the reception of this great work, **in order to raise funds for its completion,** have prepared a miniature Statuette *six inches in height,*—the Statue Bronzed; Pedestal, Nickel-silvered,—which they are now delivering to subscribers throughout the United States at **One Dollar Each.**

This attractive souvenir and Mantel or Desk ornament is a *perfect fac-simile* of the model furnished by the artist.

The Statuette in same metal, *twelve inches high,* at **Five Dollars Each,** delivered.

The designs of Statue and Pedestal are protected by U. S. Patents, and the models can *only* be furnished by *this Committee.* Address, with remittance,

RICHARD BUTLER, Secretary,
American Committee of the Statue of Liberty,
33 Mercer Street, New-York.

While the French collected 400,000 francs for the Statue, Americans raised money for her pedestal through newspapers, right, and selling souvenirs. A newspaper ad, left, announces miniatures for sale, similar to the one on page 29; above, a commemorative medal of the sculptor. **BELOW** *A plaque on the monument with the sculptor and foundry's names.*

PLEASE MAIL COPY OF YOUR PAPER CONTAINING NOTICE.

Liberty Enlightening the World.

This new Wonder of the World, which is now being loaded on the French transport Isère for shipment to this country, is the largest statue in the world. Some idea of its magnitude may be obtained from the fact that forty persons found standing-room within the head. A six-foot man standing on the level of the lips only just reached the eyebrow. While workmen were employed on the crown of her head they seemed to be making a huge sugar-caldron, and they jumped with ease in and out the tip of the nose. Fifteen people might sit round the flame of the torch, which elevation can be reached by a spiral staircase within the outstretched arm.

The London *Daily News*, in speaking of it, says: "It is out and away the largest statue of modern times. The Colossus of Rhodes was nothing to it. It could carry the 'Bravaria' or the 'Hermann' in its arms. It towers to the skies from the yard of the Rue de Chazelles, where it has been eight years in construction, and the view from its coronet sweeps clear of the six-story houses and beyond the walls of Paris."

The weight of this stupendous statue is 440,000 pounds, of which 176,000 pounds are copper and the remainder wrought-iron. It is expected to arrive in New York about the 25th of May, where it will be erected on Bedloe's Island, this being the location selected for it by Gen. W. T. Sherman, who was appointed by the President to make the selection. When placed in position it will loom up 305 feet above tide-water, the height of the statue being 151.2 feet, that of the pedestal 91 feet, and foundation 52.10 feet.

This imposing statue, higher than the enormous towers of the great Brooklyn Bridge or the steeple of Trinity Church, which is the loftiest in the city of New York,—higher, in fact, than any of the colossal statues of antiquity,—by its rare artistic proportions, as well as by its stupendous dimensions, will add another to the Wonders of the World. A word should be said of its artistic merit. The pose, stride, and gesture, with its classic face, are pronounced perfect; the drapery is both massive and fine, and in some parts is as delicate and silky in effect as if wrought with a fine chisel on the smallest scale.

The conception and execution of this great work are due to the great French sculptor, M. Bartholdi, who has devoted eight years of his life and most of his fortune to this great work, and whose generous impulses, which must be on a scale commensurate with this noble work, prompted him to make such a gift to the United States. The committee in charge of the construction of the base and pedestal for the reception of this great work are in want of funds for its completion, and have prepared a miniature statuette, an exact counterpart of the original, six inches in height, the figure being made of bronze, the pedestal of nickel silver, which they are now delivering to subscribers throughout the United States for the small sum of $1 each. Aside from its being a lasting souvenir of this colossal statue, it will ornament our homes and bear testimony that we have contributed to the completion of one of the grandest works of modern times. All remittances should be addressed to Richard Butler, Secretary American Committee of the Statue of Liberty, No. 33 Mercer Street, New York. The committee are also prepared to furnish a model, in same metals, twelve inches in height, at $5 each, delivered.

We feel assured our people will be only too eager to testify their grateful sense of the friendliness of this magnanimous offer on the part of the French people, and to reciprocate the kindly and liberal sentiments in which it originated, by thus aiding in an active prosecution of the labors that may be required to give the statue an appropriate base and pedestal. Now is the time to do it. Whoever wishes to have the honor and pleasure of contributing to the erection of the grandest statue of any age, to say nothing of the sentiment that should be welcomed and encouraged, must act promptly, for the money will be raised as sure as the sun rises. Every subscriber sending $1 will be supplied with a miniature counterpart of this great and imperishable statue of

"LIBERTY ENLIGHTENING THE WORLD."

Courtesy of SOL-EIF, Inc. / Pulitzer Foundation.

The pedestal fund found a champion in Joseph Pulitzer, left, owner of The New York World. *Wanting to serve the public interest—and attract new readers—Pulitzer launched a campaign in his newspaper to raise the final monies needed for the structure. He promised to publish the name of every donor, "no matter how small the sum given". Children by the thousands sent in their allowances and, in return, received a pin signifying membership in the paper's "Kiddie Klub," above. The campaign ended when it reached its goal of $100,000, only five months after it started.*

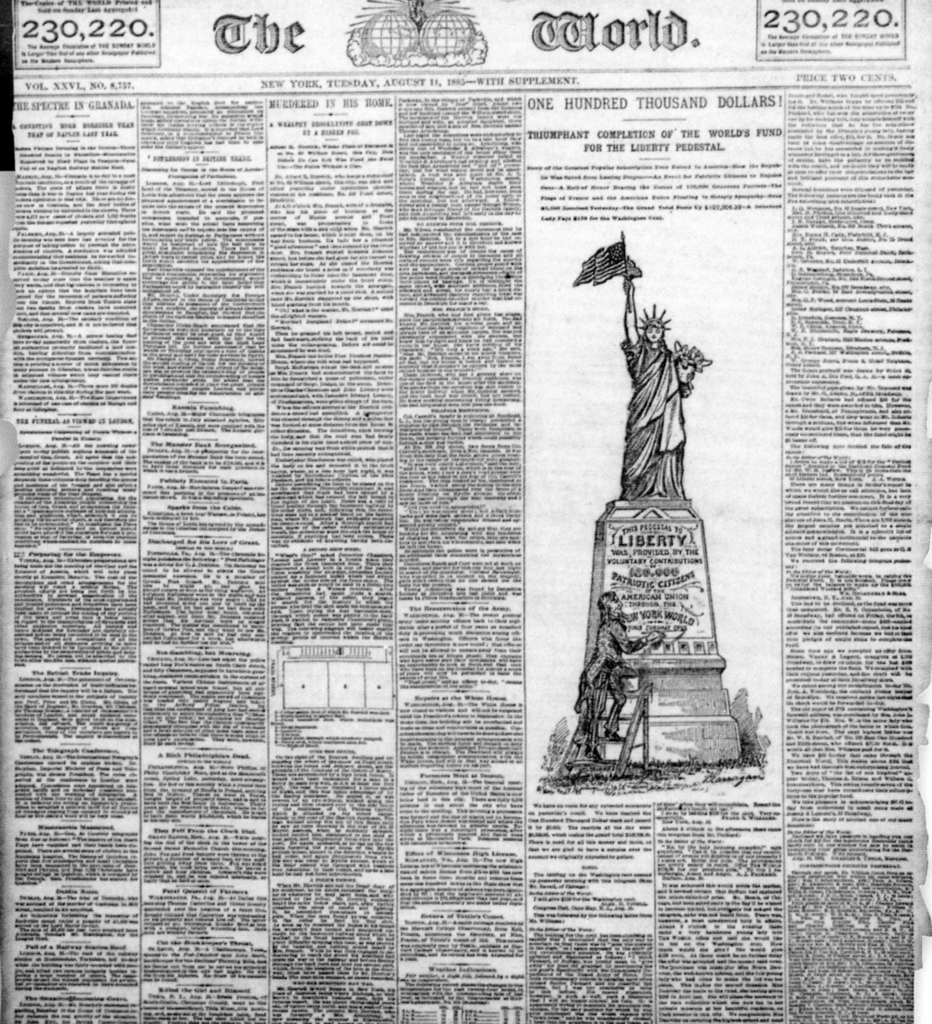

230,220.

The World.

230,220.

VOL. XXVI., NO. 8,757. NEW YORK, TUESDAY, AUGUST 11, 1885—WITH SUPPLEMENT. PRICE TWO CENTS.

THE SPECTRE IN GRANADA.

MURDERED IN HIS HOME.

ONE HUNDRED THOUSAND DOLLARS!

TRIUMPHANT COMPLETION OF THE WORLD'S FUND FOR THE LIBERTY PEDESTAL.

THIS PEDESTAL TO LIBERTY WAS PROVIDED BY THE VOLUNTARY CONTRIBUTIONS OF 120,000 PATRIOTIC CITIZENS OF THE AMERICAN UNION THROUGH THE NEW YORK WORLD

Collection of the New-York Historical Society

More than 100 years after the Statue was completed, children continue to love the Lady. Here a special visitor from the "Make a Wish Foundation" gets a bird's eye view of the torch during the restoration.

LEFT *A cutaway of the monument showing its inner support system.* **ABOVE** *A rare 1882 photograph of the Statue undergoing construction outside the Paris foundry of Gaget, Gauthier et Companie, fabricators of decorative metalwork. For almost 10 years—until the Statue was completed in 1884—Parisians watched Liberty take shape. As the Statue grew taller, workers entered the structure through the right heel, opposite page, the only copper "skin" not set in place until the Statue was reassembled in America.*

Eiffel designs the structure

The immense size of the Statue—151′1″ in height—necessitated an inner support system that was revolutionary, so Bartholdi called upon engineer Alexandre-Gustave Eiffel, above, for help. Although Eiffel had not yet built the tower for which he would become famous, he had developed a reputation throughout Europe for designing innovative railroad bridges. For Bartholdi's imposing copper Statue, he devised a structural support based on a central pylon composed of four wrought-iron columns that bear the weight. Attached to the pylon is a vast interior strap-work that supports the copper skin.

Collection of the New-York Historical Society

PRECEDING PAGES *Vestiges of star-shaped Ft. Wood as seen from a window in the Statue's crown.* **ABOVE** *Foundation for the pedestal undergoing construction on Bedloe's Island. Rising 53 feet above an abandoned fort, the concrete structure formed the pedestal's base.* **BELOW** *Perpetuating a tradition that dates from antiquity, Masons assemble to lay a cornerstone in the foundation during a rain-soaked ceremony in August of 1884.* **RIGHT** *Silver trowel used in the ceremony.*

Collection of the New-York Historical Society

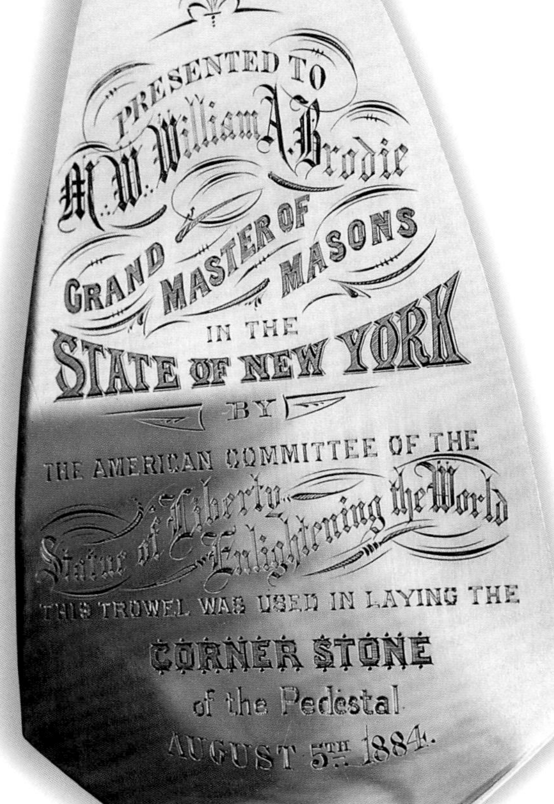

ABOVE *Commemorating the 100th anniversary of the first ceremony, Masons gather again at the Statue, by chance on another rainy day. The Masons were major contributors to the reconstruction and had their own special pin, at right.*

Made of concrete faced with granite, the 89-foot pedestal was designed by Richard Morris Hunt, the most fashionable American architect of his day. **ABOVE LEFT** *Round, ornamental escutcheons-40 in all-were once intended to bear the coats of arms of the forty states that made up the Union in 1886. Other architectural features include rough and smooth stone work, at left, and a pillared loggia, or gallery, opposite.*

Granger Collection

In mapping out our strategy, we wanted to include the whole country in the project—even those who had never seen the Statue up close. And that's where photographer Peter B. Kaplan played a part. Almost weekly, we released a story on the restoration's progress—always accompanied by a Kaplan photo and an address for where to send donations. Soon the wire services, newspapers, and magazines, both here and abroad, ran our story.

Mail began pouring in by the bag loads. Most envelopes contained a check or a few dollar bills. Some contained plays, artwork, poems or original songs. And almost all had a letter that told of a personal connection with the Lady in the Harbor.

She was there to bid good-by to the soldiers on their way to war, and to welcome them upon their return. She was there for the young bride sailing to Europe on her honeymoon, and for the schoolgirl on a summer vacation. She was there for the refugee fleeing oppression in a far-off land and for the children born under her shadow. And she was there for the millions of immigrants who landed at nearby Ellis Island.

As I discovered in reading these letters, the Statue means many things to many people. Liberty is a friend, an ally, a symbol of an ideal that cannot die—democracy. She is hope, She is freedom, She is America.

No wonder a lot of patriots came forward to help when they found out She was in trouble.

OPPOSITE *Immigrants arriving in New York Harbor at the turn of the century as portrayed in this drawing from* Frank Leslie's Illustrated Newspaper. *Later the popular illustration was reproduced on a variety of objects including the Staffordshire bowl at right. Over time, the Statue became closely identified with the immigrant experience, thanks in part to Emma Lazarus's poem, "The New Colossus".* **ABOVE** *One of the first souvenir pamphlets sold at the Statue.* **FOLLOWING PAGES** *"Liberté mon Amour," photographed with a pole-mounted camera.*

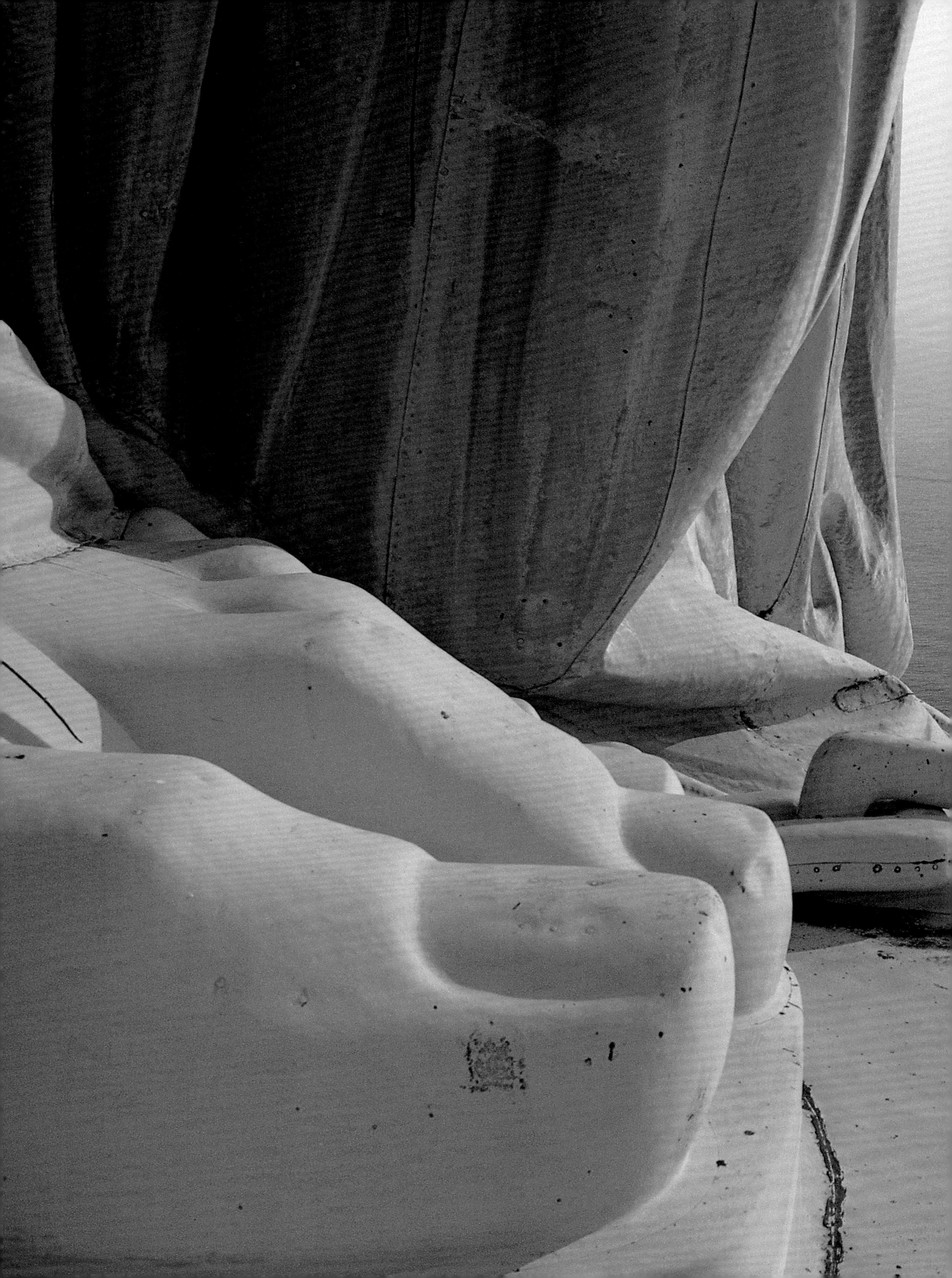

Chapter 2

America's Symbol

If there's one thing I've learned, you can't please everybody even when you share the same goal.

From day one I was worried that we wouldn't be able to raise enough money to fix the Statue, so we had a lot of cards up our sleeve: we pitched our campaign in the mail; we solicited foundations; we organized a grassroots campaign; we licensed products; we even got the Treasury Department to mint special coins. But when we approached corporations to help pay for the Statue's makeover, boy did some members of the New York press howl—commercialism!!

But that didn't stop us. We needed pledges from corporate America so we could sign contracts, begin construction and, more importantly, pay up when the job was done. Unlike Washington, which often authorizes a project and then never gets around to funding it, we couldn't wait forever to start. Not if we were to bring the project in on time.

Several sponsors came onboard during the early months. Eventually the number grew to twenty. These companies were allowed to use the Foundation's

continued on page 57

PRECEDING PAGES *Shackles of oppression and tyranny lie broken at the feet of Liberty. For more than 100 years she has proclaimed the ideals of democracy around the world.* **OPPOSITE** *The Statue's image placed by protesters at a makeshift shrine in front of the Chinese Embassy in Washington, D.C., during the 1989 Tiananmen Square uprising.*

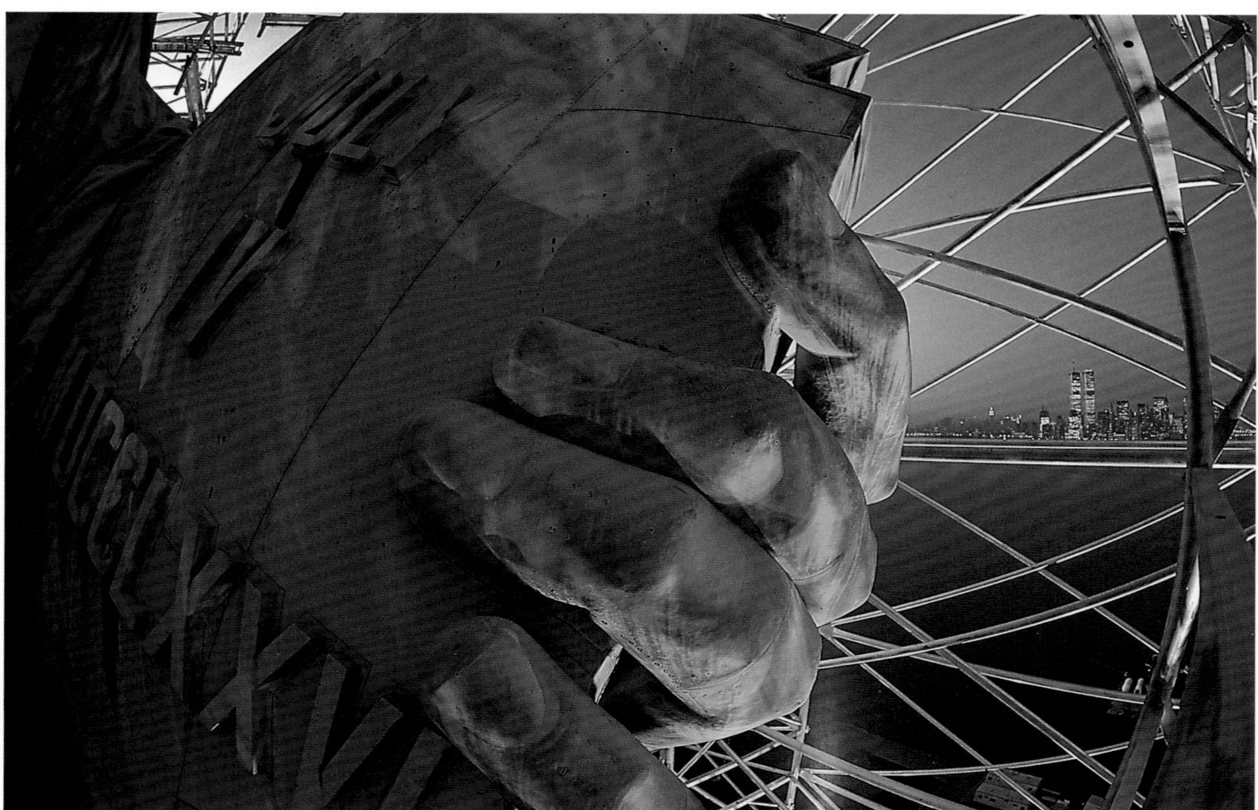

TOP *A symbol of enlightenment: the Statue's torch, seen here pre-restoration.* **BOTTOM** *The tablet she carries bears the date of American Independence, July 4, 1776.* **OPPOSITE** *Her rays represent the seven continents and seven seas.* **FOLLOWING PAGES** *Extreme close-up of Liberty's torch-bearing hand.*

ABOVE *A copper paperweight and calendar: on the reverse side, words from the "New Colossus". As Liberty's popularity grew, the use of her image in a variety of forms and contexts brought Bartholdi's statue a celebrity unparalleled by any other work in its day.*

OPPOSITE *For millions of newcomers who landed at Ellis Island, the Statue represented a new world filled with opportunity and hope.* **ABOVE** *Emma Lazarus's poem set to music by Irving Berlin, an immigrant from Russia.* **RIGHT** *An anti-immigration cartoon.*

Granger Collection

THEY FIGHT FOR YOU
PROTECT THEM
HELP THE RED CROSS
RAISE $100,000,000 AT ONCE

logo in their advertising campaigns. Some made outright donations; others made pledges to be paid out over time. Bottom line—their commitment meant we could begin.

Ironically, the Statue's sculptor, Frédéric-Auguste Bartholdi, was the first to use Liberty's image to raise money. Although the monument was a gift from the French people to America on the nation's 100th birthday, it took almost ten years to fund her construction. To help pay for his monument, Bartholdi, for a fee, allowed French companies to use her image in their ads. Now, here we were almost a hundred years later, being criticized for doing the same thing that helped bring about the Statue in the first place. Sometimes you can't win. Bring business into the picture and you "commercialize" things. Bring government in, and you "politicize" them.

Since I was a child, the Statue has played an important role in my family. It was the first American landmark my father, Nicola, saw when he arrived from Italy in 1902 at the age of 12—poor and alone. I often wonder what he felt when he sailed into the harbor, looked out, and saw the Lady? Was he scared, anxious, excited? He probably felt all of this and more. And like millions of other immigrants, he came with little more than the clothes on his back and a dream of a better life.

Poets say the Statue symbolized hope for the immigrant, and Ellis Island, the reality. I know it did for my father. Ellis Island was where people stopped being foreigners and started being Americans. As these immigrants spread out across the land, they worked hard to succeed

continued on page 62

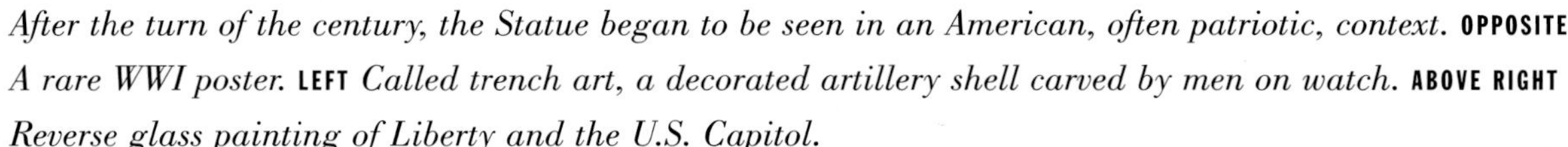

After the turn of the century, the Statue began to be seen in an American, often patriotic, context. **OPPOSITE** *A rare WWI poster.* **LEFT** *Called trench art, a decorated artillery shell carved by men on watch.* **ABOVE RIGHT** *Reverse glass painting of Liberty and the U.S. Capitol.*

ABOVE *Manufacturers such as Spalding imprinted Liberty's image to market their products.*

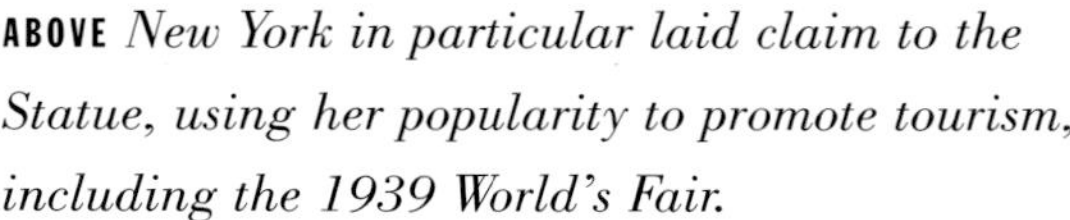

ABOVE *New York in particular laid claim to the Statue, using her popularity to promote tourism, including the 1939 World's Fair.*

Advertisers seized upon her public domain status. **RIGHT** *A special bottle of Jim Beam whisky, now a collector's item.*

ABOVE *WWII victory postcard featuring tanks and planes used during the war.* **RIGHT** *Memento from Dachau, the German postcard marks the liberation of the concentration camp.*

LEFT *A WWI Emerson record featuring the Metropolitan Military Band playing "Trilby Rag."*

BELOW *A WW II poster exhorting stevedores to work quickly.*

Cortesy Museum of the City of New York

ABOVE *Soldiers returning from war greet their favorite lady in a cartoon of the day.*
RIGHT *Song sheet for a WWII ode to French-American friendship.*

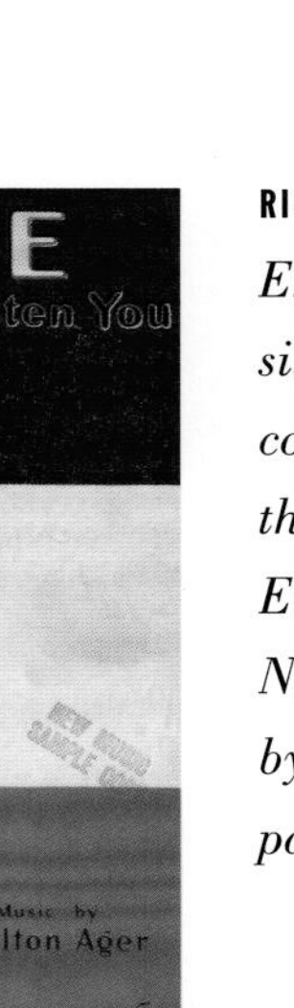

ABOVE *A special Statue Pin created after the attack on Pearl Harbor.*

RIGHT *Made in England, a silver pin commemorates the liberation of Europe and North Africa by American paratroopers.*

Just as Liberty's image found its way into popular American culture, it also inspired replicas to spring up both here and abroad. **ABOVE** *A Boy Scout memorial in Loveland, Colorado, set against the Rocky Mountains.* **LEFT TOP** *A topiary monument in Cape May, New Jersey.*

LEFT CENTER *A statue made of Legos.* **LEFT BOTTOM** *Pizza parlor in Las Vegas.* **RIGHT TOP** *Luxembourg Gardens in Paris, France.* **RIGHT CENTER** *Wall art in Brooklyn.* **RIGHT BOTTOM** *A Wichita, Kansas Boy Scout memorial at a local high school.* **INSET** *Scout pin, left, and kerchief slide.*

and finally to belong to their adopted country. And so also was America changed by them. They fueled our industry, enriched our culture and settled our cities and towns.

Ironically, this association of the Statue with the immigrant experience didn't occur to most people at first. I did a little research and discovered that except for a brief mention in the *New York Herald* on the day the Statue was dedicated, it wasn't until several years later that people connected her to the newcomers flooding America's shores. Only a young unknown poet named Emma Lazarus back in the 1880s put the two together. She wrote a poem "The New Colossus", which was eventually placed on the Statue's pedestal. Later, Irving Berlin, an Ellis Island immigrant, set her words to music in his song "Give Me Your Tired, Your Poor".

It didn't take long after the Statue opened for it to become a familiar New York landmark and popular tourist attraction. Eventually she became synonymous with America itself. Her image popped up everywhere: in editorial cartoons, on posters, in ads, and on company logos.

Today, the Statue is not just an American icon, but also the foremost symbol of freedom around the globe. But symbols mean nothing if the values aren't there. We didn't spend millions on the Statue so she wouldn't fall into the harbor and become a hazard to navigation, or so she would become a nice place to picnic on a Sunday afternoon. We did it because we wanted to restore, remember, and renew the basic values that made America great.

I discovered that a lot of other people felt the same way.

OPPOSITE *One of the most popular tourist attractions in America, the Statue draws upwards of three million visitors annually. Wear and tear on the monument over the years prompted a major restoration that was completed in time to celebrate its 100th anniversary in 1986. Souvenirs: an enamel pin and a sterling silver spoon.* **FOLLOWING PAGES** *The Statue at dusk. Throughout the world, she remains the most powerful image of America—to friend and foe alike.*

Chapter 3

Restoration Begins

Where to begin. First, the obstacles.

How do you set up a construction area in the middle of one of the world's busiest harbors, without breaking the bank? And with thousands of visitors traipsing over the site each day. Believe me, it wasn't easy.

Liberty Island has always been unique. It's been a national monument since 1937. It boasts three million visitors a year. And when we started construction in 1984, it was a year-round home to several Park Service families. The only access was, and still is, by boat.

To meet the demands of the public, the Park Service, construction, and security, we had to build a separate dock just to unload equipment, materials and personnel. That meant we had to hire a boat service to ferry the workers back and forth from the Battery in lower Manhattan. And then we had to hire guards. Already our budget was feeling the strain.

In January of 1984, workers started assembling the world's tallest freestanding scaffolding. Made of aluminum, it stood 18 inches out from the Statue. It

continued on page 77

PRECEDING PAGES *Vanguard of construction, an aluminum scaffold built in 1984.* **OPPOSITE** *Life goes on—even in dead of winter—for Dave Moffitt, superintendent of the Statue during the two and one-half year restoration project. While undergoing repairs, the monument remained open to visitors for 18 months.*

ABOVE *Fundraising begins at an inaugural event in 1982. Iacocca volunteered his time to chair the Statue of Liberty-Ellis Island Foundation, a private, non-profit organization created to raise the necessary funds to restore the Statue and its companion monument, Ellis Island, and to oversee the two restoration projects.* **PRECEDING PAGES** *A rare view of the Statue shows the intricate folds of her classical Roman garb. Over time, the Statue developed its familiar green patina that protects the copper from corrosion.*

Throughout the fundraising campaign, performers from all parts of the entertainment industry donated both time and talent. **ABOVE** *Bob Hope and Luciano Pavarotti appear at a benefit held at New York's Lincoln Center. Hope wears a "Save our Statue" clip, below, one of the first campaign pins.*

Sponsors come on board

During the restoration, twenty corporations each pledged to contribute up to $5 million to save the Statue. Most developed special marketing programs including Eastman Kodak, which featured a Peter B. Kaplan photograph at New York's Grand Central Station. Early on, these advertising campaigns helped publicize the restoration to the American public.

New Haven Line
Harlem-Hudson Lines
Tickets
Harlem — Hudson — New Haven Lines

was only attached at the bottom, and when the breeze picked up, it would sway back and forth. On a windy day it could be quite unnerving if you were standing at the top, although you couldn't find a better view in all New York.

People are always asking me what it was like to work with the government. One word sums it up: interesting. Like any other relationship, we had our ups and downs. We agreed on some things, disagreed on others. Occasionally we both refused to budge an inch. But one of the reasons it worked out in our case was because of a Texan named Dave Moffitt.

Dave was the Statue's superintendent. He was also the Park Service representative at weekly Foundation meetings. Dave spoke his mind, and occasionally butted heads with Briganti and the others, but he was also practical. He knew that sometimes you have to give a little, to get a little. We were fortunate to have him involved.

continued on page 88

OPPOSITE *Aluminum rods used in the Statue's scaffold await completion of a 400-foot supply ramp, above, that led from the water's edge to the pedestal's base. The ramp and scaffold were assembled by Universal Builders Supply (UBS) of upstate New York.* **INSET** *UBS Pin.*

With the Aid of Computers

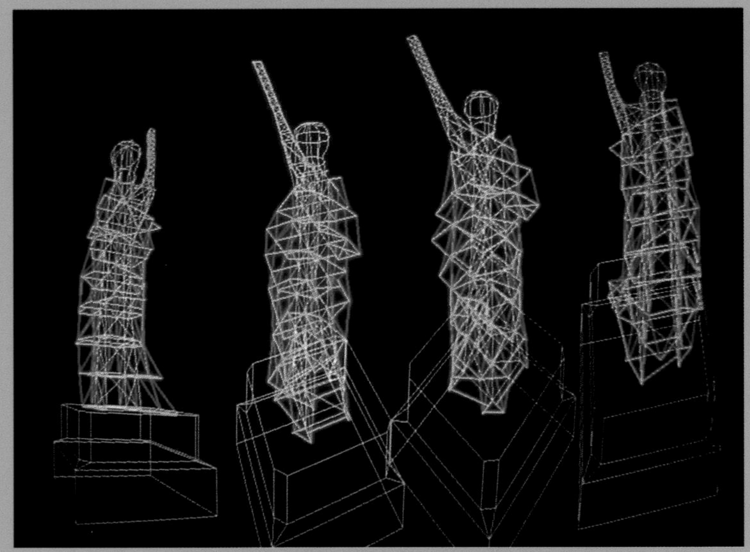

Unlike Bartholdi and Eiffel, who had to rely on trial and error to solve construction problems, the experts who consulted on the Statue's restoration used innovative technology to assist in their work. Computers were used in all phases of the project, from drawing plans to constructing models, from calculating stress on metal to staging work, from taking inventory to monitoring production schedules. The National Park Service, administrator of the monument, in cooperation with the Foundation, assembled a team of outstanding architects, engineers, artisans, and historians from both here and abroad to help on the project. Work on the monument was put out to bid, with construction companies and vendors from along the East Coast hired for the job.

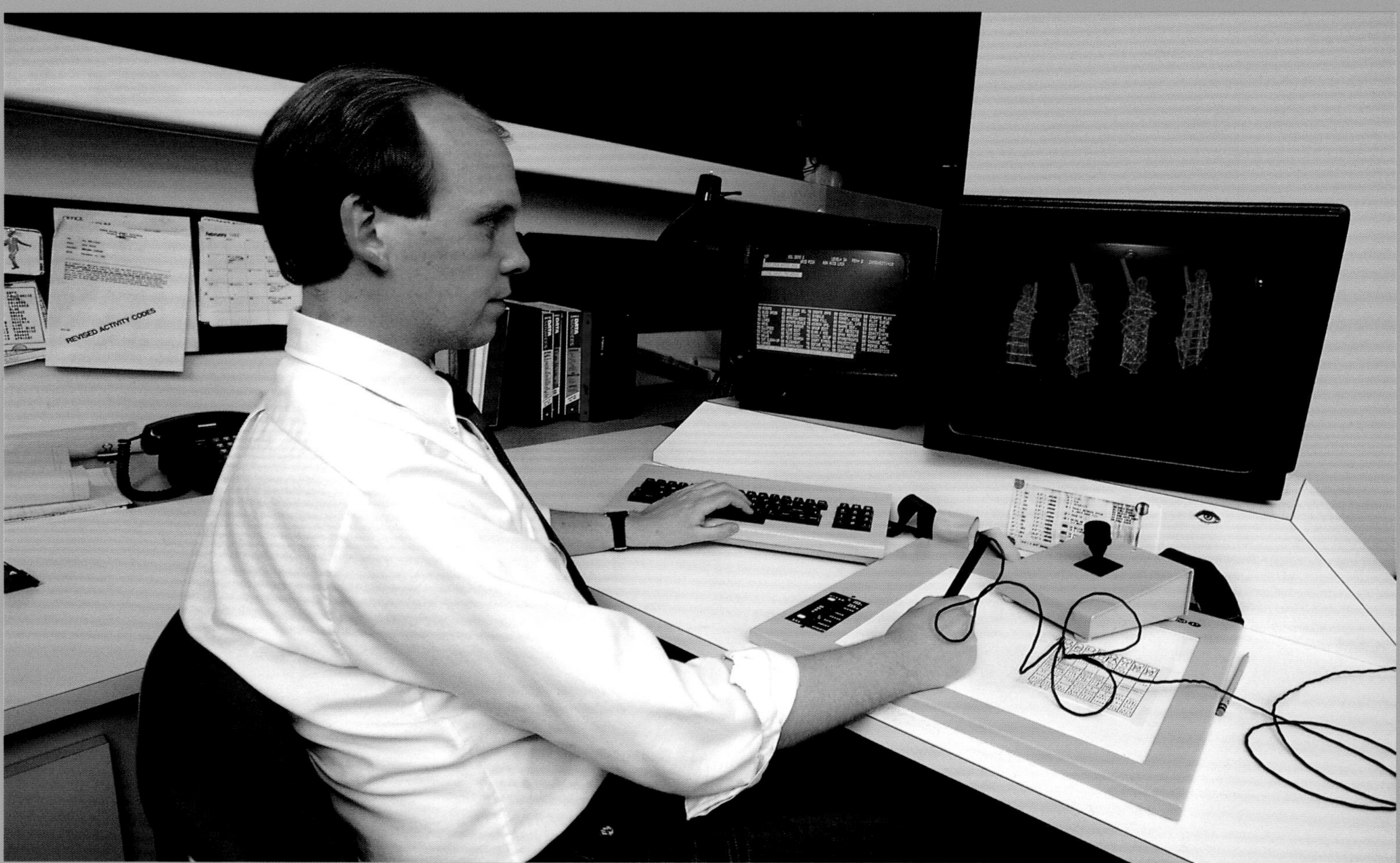

With the aid of a special program, an architectural draftsman creates a three-dimensional image of the Statue's internal support system as seen in the enlargement above. The computer-enhanced drawing illustrates the complexity and genius of Eiffel's design and also helped engineers plan repairs on the iron structure.

PAGES 78-79 *Still visible above the rising scaffolding, the Statue measures 305′1″ tall, from the ground to the top of the torch.*
PAGES 80-81 *Workers anchor the scaffolding to the monument's pedestal.*

Using a model of the Statue's structural skeleton, architect Richard Hayden examines the position of the arm. Although Eiffel planned for the Statue's main support pylon to carry its weight, the upraised arm was attached further out than intended, causing the right shoulder to weaken.

A lot of people called the restoration the project of the century. It's easy to see why. A thousand people worked four years to fix her up. For many, it became the job of a lifetime, combining skills, common sense and much ingenuity. After all, one hundred years of corrosion, weathering, pollution—not to mention all those sightseers—had taken their toll. Besides, no one had worked on a 305 ft. copper statue before—at least not in the last fifty years—so we wrote the book as we went along.

The last of the scaffold was set in place by late April of '84—a perfect time of year for a topping off ceremony and to stage a press event, one of many we would have over the next two years. Encased in 300 tons of aluminum, the Statue became an eerie presence in the harbor. And also an object of much curiosity.

We built a workshop on the island, with a viewing area behind a large glass window. There, visitors could watch workers replicate ancient techniques for molding copper. Since there were no textbooks to guide us, much of the work was by trial and error. It became an education for both worker and visitor.

Education. That's something that's very important to me. I have two daughters, and it wasn't until I became involved in the project that they saw Liberty up close. My kids had been to New York often, but to museums, to Broadway shows, to restaurants—and to shop. We did the town lots of times, but not once in all those visits, did I bring my family to the Statue. Not once did I ever say to them: It's great to be free; it's great to be an American; let's go to the Statue. In fact, I myself had never been back since my father took me many years ago. It was only after I became involved with the restoration that I visited the island again.

I thought about this a lot and then I realized that the Statue didn't mean as much to me as it did to my father. He was free to work hard and build a great life

continued on page 93

OPPOSITE *Encased in a maze of aluminum, Liberty awaits removal of her torch. Attached only at the bottom, the scaffold stood 18 inches out from the Statue on all sides to accommodate the Statue's movement during high winds.*
PAGES 84-85 *The scaffold—tallest free-standing in the world—weighed 300 tons and rose some 300 feet high, from the base of the pedestal to above the torch.* **PAGES 86-87** *Scrambling without a safety net or harness, workers easily navigate the complex structure.*

Photo taken from The Goodyear Blimp.

At a topping off ceremony in April of 1984, officials from the Foundation, the National Park Service, and construction companies unfurl the American flag as the last section of the scaffolding was completed. Throughout the restoration, sponsors, contractors, civic groups and many others created special Liberty pins like the one at right to signal their participation in the historic project.

RIGHT *Superintendent Moffitt introduces Iacocca and Foundation executive Steve Briganti to an official from the Interior Department. Iacocca actively participated in the project, not only appearing at public events that helped garner publicity, but also assuming a hands-on role as the Foundation's Chairman.*

in America and he went back to the Statue, just to say thanks in his own way. Millions like him have returned over the years, dragging kids and grandkids that didn't understand what the Statue really represents.

Liberty brings with it some obligations. We have it today because others fought for it, nourished it, protected it, and then passed it on to us. That's a debt we owe to those that have gone before. And a gift we have to pass on to future generations.

The restoration project became an opportunity to teach our children and grandchildren about America's greatest symbol of freedom—the Statue. Thanks to the help of a few educators and the *New York Daily News*, we put together some materials. For five dollars, teachers from all over the country could get a wonderful educational packet that taught about the Statue, her history, and what she represents. The paper was inundated with requests. And children everywhere wanted to SOS—"Save our Statue".

One little girl wrote me a letter. She asked, "Do you love the lady as much as I do?" My answer? "You bet. And so do millions of others."

OPPOSITE *Park Service policewoman Patty Lanario and Tally, a bomb-sniffing dog, patrol the ferry landing at Liberty Island during the restoration. Unrest in the Middle East during the 1980s prompted extra security measures even back then.* **ABOVE** *A bronze German shepherd stamped on its left shoulder with the image of the Statue, seen in the close-up at right. The souvenir is one of more than 5,000 Liberty items in the photographer's collection, the largest private holding of Statue memorabilia in the world.*

Chapter 4

A New Torch

If you visit the Statue today, she doesn't look much different than she did before the restoration, with one exception—her torch.

Bartholdi had designed his statue to carry a solid flame. Then someone got the creative idea of cutting holes in the flame, and replacing the copper with amber glass. The plan was to light it from within. Over the years rainwater seeped into the reconfigured flame, causing damage that couldn't be fixed.

The project's architects decided that the restoration was a chance to go back to Bartholdi's original concept. Using the same construction methods that built the Statue, we decided to fashion a new flame in the temporary workshop on the island. But first we needed to remove the old torch to use as a model. Not an easy task 300 feet off the ground.

It's one thing to build a skyscraper, with the crane encased within the building. As the structure gets taller, so does the crane. It's another thing to float this giant piece of equipment out on a barge, and then assemble it next to a latticework of aluminum.

continued on page 103

PRECEDING PAGES *In a race to the top, Mitch Penna from UBS beats his nearest competitor by leaps and bounds.* **OPPOSITE** *French architect Thierry Despont, in charge of designing the new flame, checks the torch.* **FOLLOWING PAGES** *Cables attached, the torch is ready to come down during a practice run for its removal.* **INSET** *An 1876 souvenir glass torch.*

Replacing Liberty's Old Flame

The restoration team decided from the beginning that the Statue's general appearance, with one exception, would be left unchanged. The only noticeable difference to the millions familiar with her image would be her new upper torch and flame. A century of modification had radically altered Bartholdi's solid copper flame, to one mainly of glass. As a result, years of rainwater leakage and corrosion had damaged the original beyond repair.

LEFT *Aided by a crane, workers remove the old torch on July 4, 1984. Remote cameras mounted on the crane above the torch recorded this event.* **ABOVE** *A scale double-checks the weight of the torch.*

No matter how many times I visited the island, it always amazed me to watch the men scamper over the scaffolding. They would leap from section to section, without giving it a second thought. Few wore safety belts. They said it inhibited them. It's a good thing our safety guys didn't see this. Our insurance costs were already through the roof. Besides, I think working on Lady Liberty brought us luck. During the entire project, we had not one major accident.

We selected July 4th, 1984 as the day for the torch removal ceremony. It would also be the kick-off for a major grassroots fundraising campaign. Two birds with one stone.

The day finally arrived, and thousands gathered on Liberty Island to watch. Unbeknownst to them, we had made a practice run the day before. We were taking no chances. With TV crews buzzing about in helicopters overhead, it wouldn't do to drop the torch in the harbor.

Lift off was successful, and that evening we made the news on all the networks. We couldn't have come up with a better publicity angle.

When we first started the campaign, I wasn't sure if we could round up enough individual contributions. And while fundraising wasn't my background, I knew we would have to appeal directly to the American public if we were to succeed. After all, it was French and American citizens who paid for the Statue in the first place. The French donated the Statue, and Americans paid for her pedestal—thanks in part to a Hungarian immigrant named Joseph Pulitzer.

Publisher of the *New York World*, Pulitzer promised to print the name of everyone who gave a donation—no matter how small—in his newspaper. And he

continued on page 115

OPPOSITE *Kicking off the Foundation's grassroots campaign, thousands gather at Liberty Island to watch the torch removal ceremony as seen from the Goodyear Blimp. Press from around the globe covered the festivities, which included a speech by Ed Koch, above, Mayor of New York.*

Working at a construction site accessible only by boat often led to boredom. Favorite pastimes—fishing for bluefish in the Hudson River and growing tomatoes—both successful in season!

Surf and Turf: Popular noontime meal of barbeque hot dogs, hamburgers and occasional fish.

Fathers and Sons

Hailed as the project of the century, the Statue's restoration employed close to a thousand people. The project was the job of a lifetime, combining finely-honed skills with common sense and much ingenuity. But for many, it also had a more personal meaning. A number of workers were descendants of immigrants and, like their fathers and grandfathers before them, worked in the building trades. It was their forebears who built the skyscrapers that line the cityscape. And it was this project that instilled in their sons and grandsons a sense of pride. For the newer generations, it became a very real way to say thank you to those who came before.

One such family was the Michilli's. Some 50 years ago, Giuseppe Michilli immigrated to America from Italy. **ABOVE** As a young father, he brought his sons, Angelo, at left, and Raphael, to see the Statue—a familiar pilgrimage for many immigrants. For Giuseppe, she represented a marvel of construction as well as a symbol of America and the opportunities it offered. Years later the family would pose at the monument for another group photo, at right. Both father and sons worked on the restoration.

The Statue's restoration generated much interest both in New York and throughout the country. At first workers used a temporary shop, at left, before building a bigger facility (below) that included a visitor's gallery. There, the public could view the restoration in progress, including the intricate fashioning of the new torch. The 4500 square foot building was built by a crew that included a Mohawk Indian, at right, from upstate New York.

Southern Baptist Church
PRAISE The LORD!
HENRI

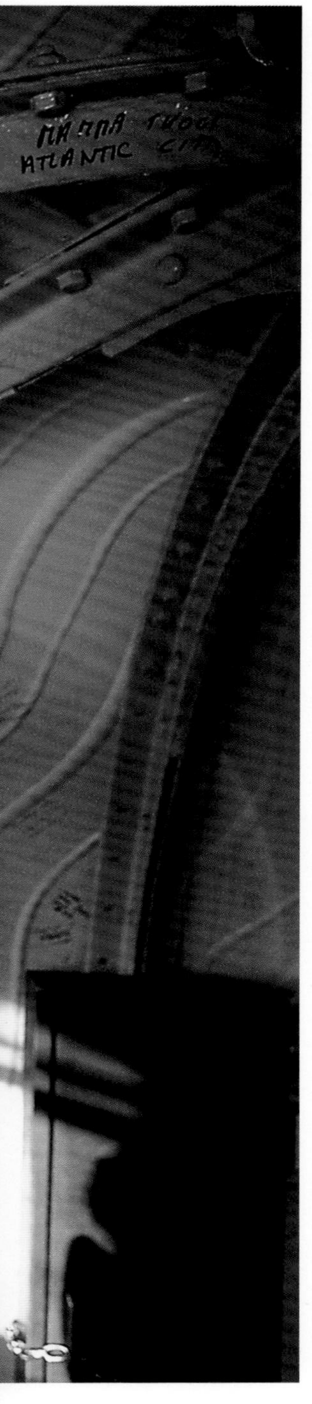

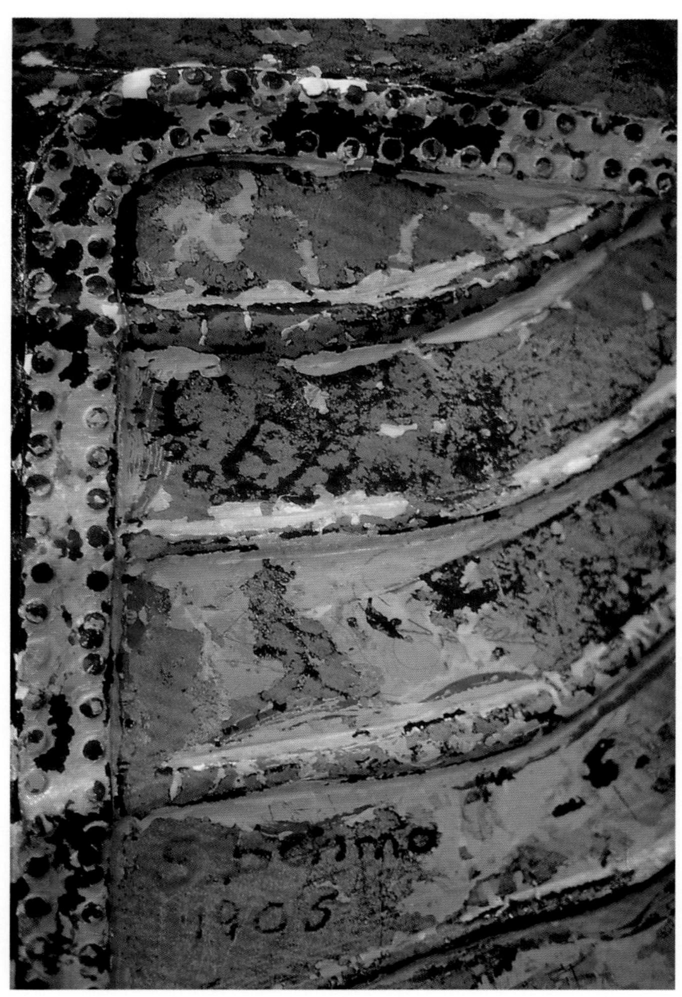

Since 1981, the Statue's physical condition had been under investigation by experts, including preservation specialists from the National Park Service, under whose care the Statue was placed in 1937. A century of corrosion, weathering, pollution and millions of sightseers had taken their toll. **OPPOSITE PAGE** *Graffiti, the bane of urban monuments, mars the inside of the Statue's head.* **LEFT** *After removing several layers of paint, still more marks are revealed, including a visitor's name dating back almost 100 years.* **BELOW** *Peeling paint and rusted iron under a stairwell in the Statue.*

TOP *Clouds rise from cold liquid nitrogen (lowered to minus 325 degrees F.) hitting the warm copper in the Statue's Crown Room.* **ABOVE** *The reaction of the cold chemical against the metal blasted off seven layers of paint from inside the Statue's face.* **RIGHT** *Paint removal within the close confines of the Statue's right arm. The ladder in the foreground leads to the torch.*

Conventional Problems, Unconventional Solutions

The magnitude and challenge of the restoration was never more evident than when it came to removing asbestos, seven layers of paint and two or three of coal tar from the inside of the Statue's skin. The coatings were applied over the years as stopgap measures to prevent leakage and corrosion. Conventional removal methods posed a risk to the copper and the possibility of explosion in the close confines of the Statue. Workers also had to be protected from the lead-based paint. They experimented with a variety of chemicals for paint removal before settling on liquid nitrogen cooled to –325° F. The tar proved more difficult. When trial blasting with crushed walnut shells and ground corn husks failed, the restoration team tried another remedy—old fashioned bicarbonate of soda, below, normally used to settle the stomach. In addition to being effective, it was a gentle abrasive.

ABOVE *Dressed in protective gear, a worker sprays baking soda on the coal tar.* **BELOW** *Scraping paint from the interior support near the Statue's mouth and nose.*

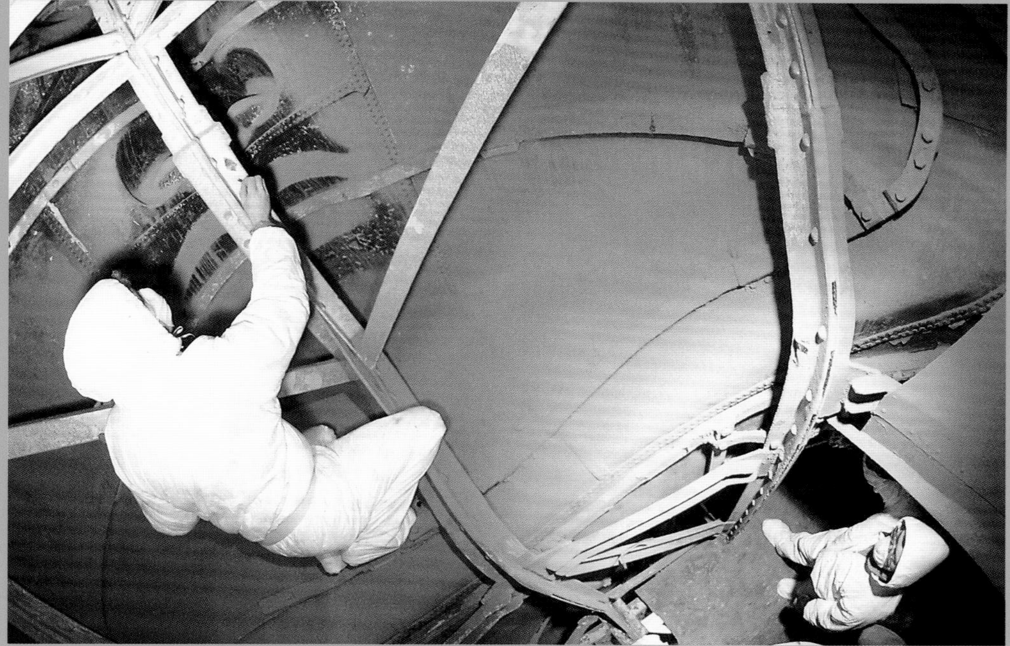

OPPOSITE *Frequent wash-downs used a special $150,000 machine that pumped water some 300 feet up from the ground.* **BELOW** *A worker sweeps off crushed walnut shells and corn husks used during an earlier attempt to eliminate the tar inside the Statue.*

ABOVE *Baking soda used to remove the tar inside the monument seeps outside, necessitating a daily cleaning to protect the Statue's patina. On some surfaces, an early black phase of the natural patina process shows through the later green state—a combination of weathering and acid rain. Experts decided against treatment of these areas so as not to damage the original copper.*

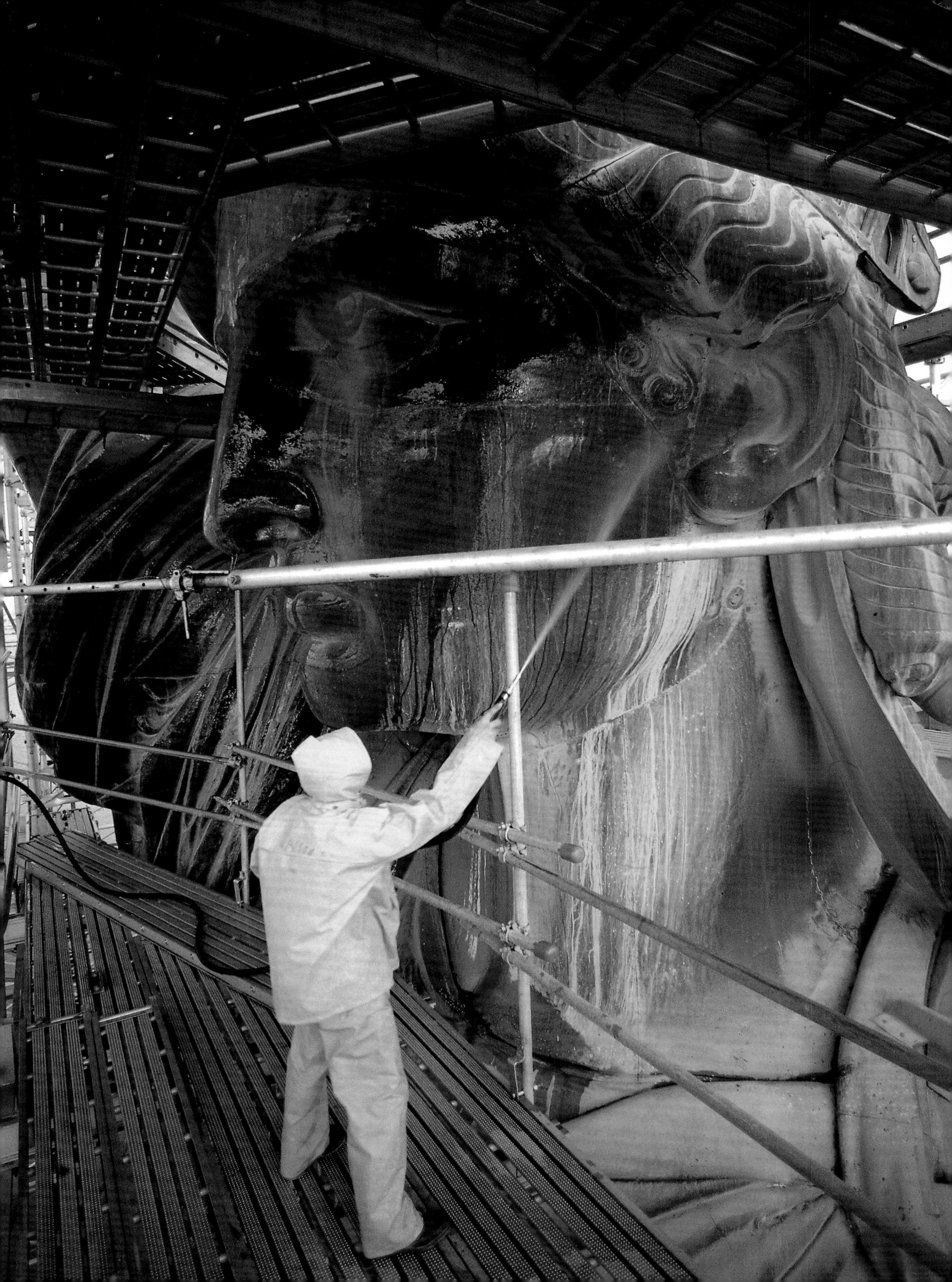

Removal of the crown's rays: Ranging up to nine feet in length and weighing some 150 pounds, each spike was examined, repaired and reinforced before being reattached.

didn't hesitate to use the bully pulpit of his paper to write editorials that lambasted the rich for not helping the cause. In the end, however, it was ordinary people that gave the bulk of the money. A hundred years later, history repeated itself.

While businesses had been generous, most of the funds to restore the Statue and Ellis Island would come from individuals. I was never disappointed. And I was always surprised.

Early on, a man walked into my office out of the blue and handed me a check for a million bucks. " You can keep it, but only on one condition—that you agree right now never to use my name."

He had come to America as a young boy and worked hard. Now a millionaire, he wanted to give back something to his adopted country. I must have told that story a thousand times as I went around the country raising money. In my speeches, I always promised that I'd keep anonymous anyone else who wanted to give a spare million. I never got another taker. But I did get a lot of money in smaller denominations. These gifts had just as much meaning.

One day a letter arrived from Poland, which was then part of the Soviet bloc. Inside, it contained two US dollars and a note from a man living under Communist rule. The money was for "this beautiful symbol". He wrote he wanted to be free some day to come to America. I don't know if his dream ever came true, but if it did, I'm pretty sure he headed straight for New York and the Lady.

When I first took on this job of raising money, I thought I had an impossible task. In the end, I never had an easier sale.

Beneath the Statue's hand, workers carry one of the rays to a construction elevator for the 295 ft. ride to the ground.

With the restoration garnering worldwide attention by the media, Greenpeace seized the opportunity to make a statement for nuclear disarmament. Navigating a labyrinth of aluminum, protesters scaled the scaffold to hang the banner at right. A sign of calmer times: New York City police, below, took the trespassers and their actions in stride. **OPPOSITE** *The morning sun casts a glow where Liberty's torch once shined.*

Liberty's Flame on Tour

With the removal of the original flame—slated to be part of the new museum in the Statue—officials at the Park Service and Foundation decided to tour the historic structure, a decision that echoed the exhibition of the torch in Philadelphia more than a hundred years ago. For the first time, many Americans were able to see a part of the Statue they had only viewed in pictures. This up close and personal tour aided fundraising across the country. No longer just a New York project, the Statue's restoration was now an American cause.

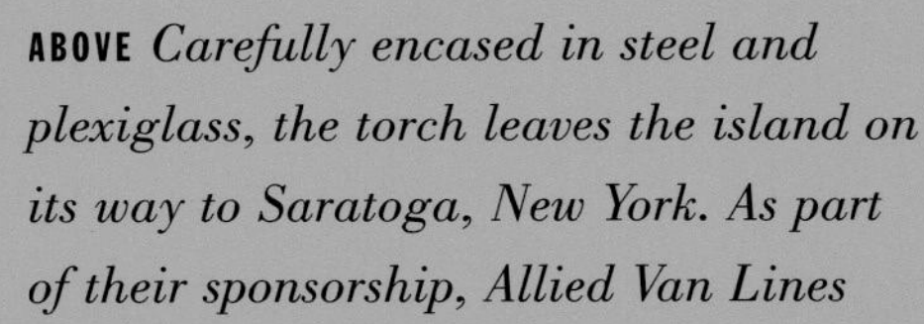

ABOVE *Carefully encased in steel and plexiglass, the torch leaves the island on its way to Saratoga, New York. As part of their sponsorship, Allied Van Lines trucked the torch to various cities.* **RIGHT** *Greeted with a trumpeter playing "God Bless America," the torch returns home from its first tour, which included an appearance in the 96th Rose Bowl Parade in Pasadena, California. Special pins, left, commemorate the event.*

ABOVE *Heading for Brooklyn, the torch casts a bright glow at the start of its historic off-island journey.* **FOLLOWING PAGES** *The Statue encased in scaffolding, an imposing presence on the waterfront.*

Chapter 5

Interior Restoration

We sent the Statue on tour. Or at least a part of her.

Someone came up with the idea of carting the old torch across America so people could see the Statue up close and be part of history. Not to mention chip in a few bucks for the cause.

Carefully encased in a special box, the weathered flame became an important part of our campaign. It appeared in parades and other major events. We even had a slogan—"Keep the Torch Lit"—that popped up on t-shirts, coffee mugs, and dozens of other licensed items, all of which could be purchased for a modest fee. We needed to keep that money rolling in. By now, our costs were soaring!

Despite the good intentions of all concerned—the Foundation, the Park Service and dozens of architects, engineers and construction managers—to hold firm to our budget, there were some things we couldn't avoid. We were charting new territory.

continued on page 142

PRECEDING PAGES *Structural Iron Workers from Local 40 cut away steel beams to install a new passenger elevator, part of the interior renovation in the Statue.* **OPPOSITE** *Fabrice Sassenus climbs a smaller bronze version of Bartholdi's monument on an island in the middle of the Seine River in Paris. Americans living in the French city during the 1880's donated the sculpture. In the background, the Eiffel Tower, named after its builder, whose genius created the support for the world's tallest statue.* **INSET** *French Statue pins.*

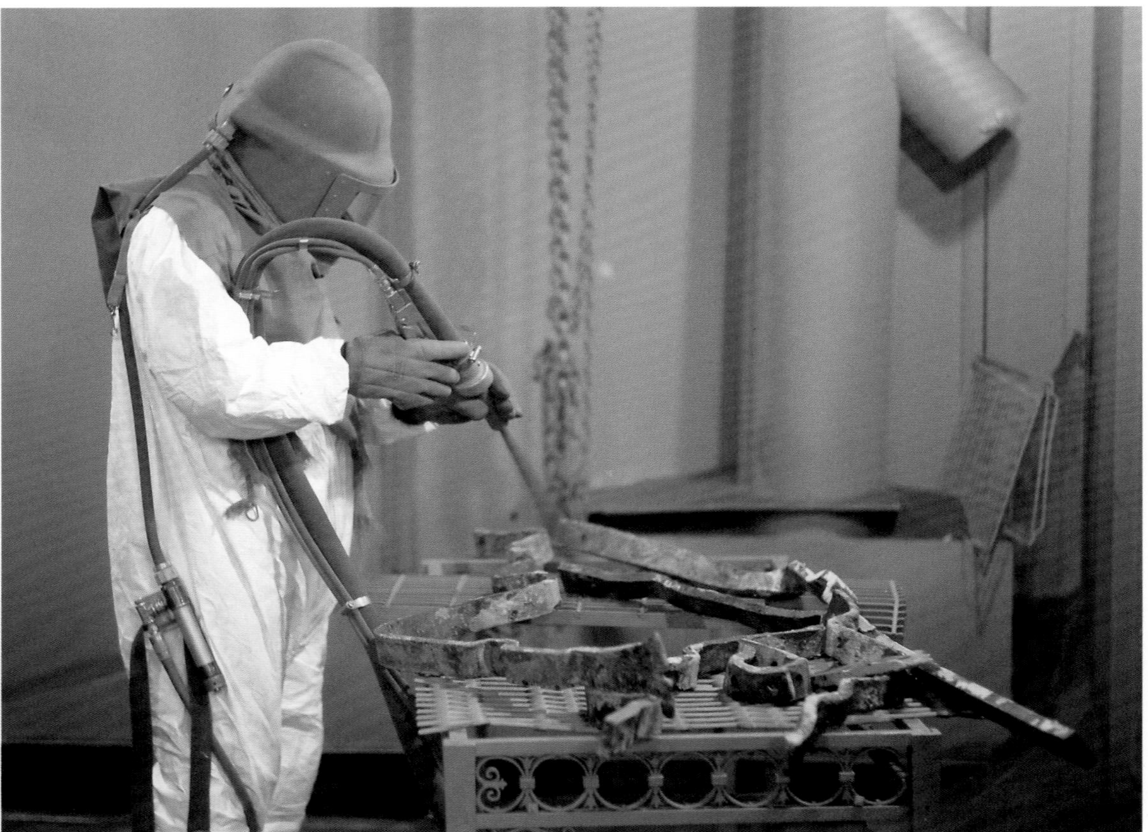

ABOVE LEFT *A worker in disposable protective gear, scrapes asbestos backing off an armature bar, one of some 1800 that supports the Statue's skin.* **ABOVE RIGHT** *A steel hammer chips away at the remaining paint. The numbered tag denotes the bar's exact location inside the Statue.* **BOTTOM** *Sandblasting gives a final cleaning before the bar is replicated.* **OPPOSITE** *Using an original bar as a pattern, skilled hands guide a high-powered saw to make a duplicate bar from stainless steel.*

Black & Decker
PROFESSIONAL

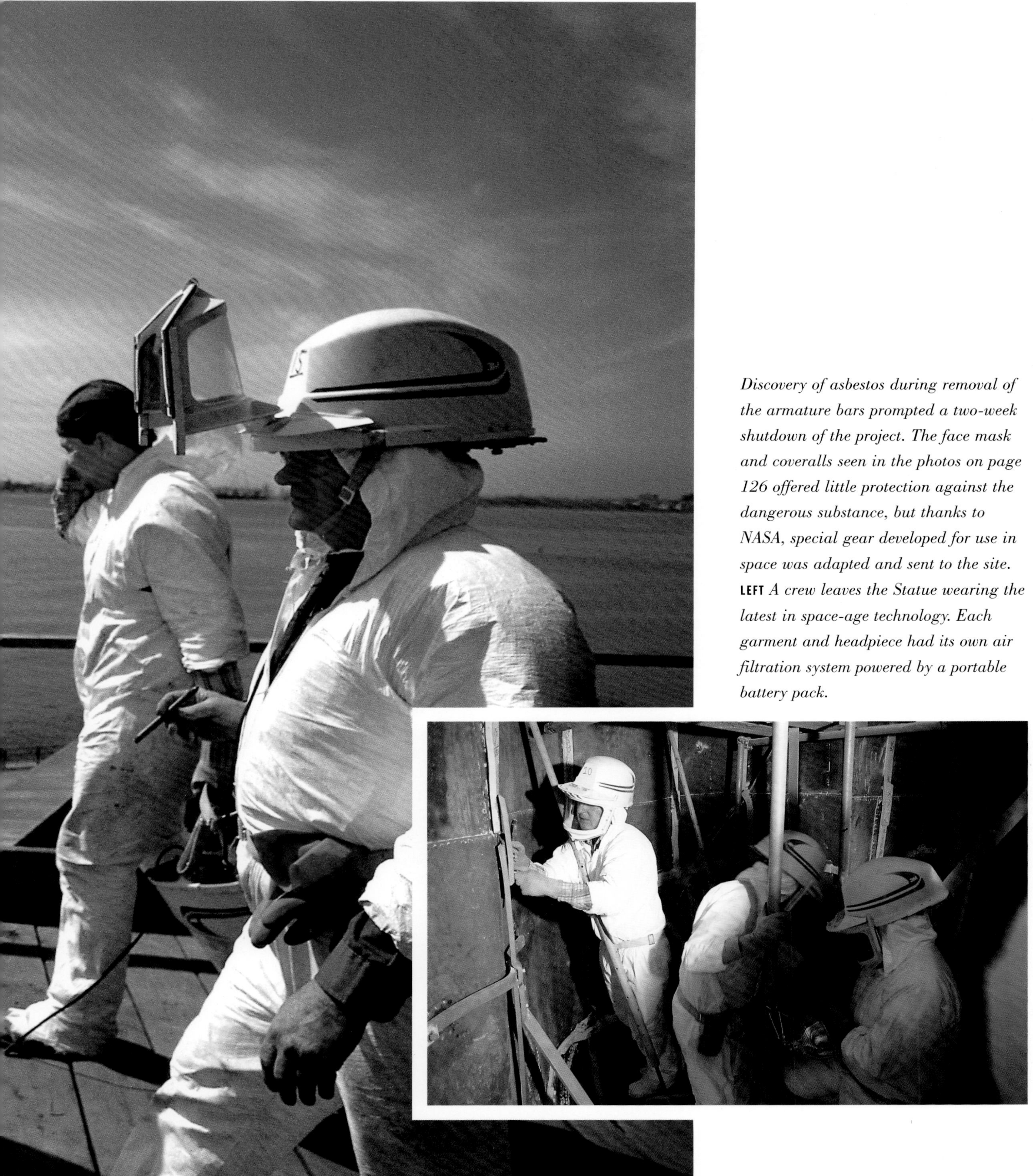

Discovery of asbestos during removal of the armature bars prompted a two-week shutdown of the project. The face mask and coveralls seen in the photos on page 126 offered little protection against the dangerous substance, but thanks to NASA, special gear developed for use in space was adapted and sent to the site.
LEFT *A crew leaves the Statue wearing the latest in space-age technology. Each garment and headpiece had its own air filtration system powered by a portable battery pack.*

PAGES 130-131 *Craftsmen from P.A. Fiebiger of New York City shape a new armature bar by hand.* **INSET** *Using the original bar for a pattern, members of Ornamental Iron Workers 580 compare new with old.*

Daily visitors to the workshop on Liberty Island watch ongoing construction. **TOP** *A worker from NAB uses a machine-like vise to bend a new piece of armature. Based in College Point, New York, NAB formed a joint venture with P. A. Fiebiger to replace all the armature bars. Fiebiger also repaired holes in the Statue's curls, nose, eyes, skin, and chain.* **ABOVE LEFT** *A worker carefully enters the number and location stamped on a new bar, at right, in his book.*
RIGHT *Ornamental Iron Workers' pin.*

Clamped in an electric vise on top of fire-proof bricks, a new bar is heated to 1905°F for two minutes, then cooled. This annealing process strengthened each piece of armature.

At night, the newly-formed bars were taken from the island workshop to Group Research in Manhattan, where they underwent an acid bath. **TOP** *Under the supervision of Richie Smith, left, Steve Weintraub backs the bars with a strip of 3-M material. This backing acted as a buffer against the Statue's skin.* **ABOVE** *Each morning, the finished bars, wrapped in plastic, returned to the island.*

RIGHT *Inside the Statue, a worker sets in place the only split armature bar above the Statue's nose, with the two pieces going to the left and right eyes. The special bar was hand forged at P.A. Fiebiger's Manhattan workshop, below. The third generation coppersmith firm fashioned the more difficult armature bars off-island.*

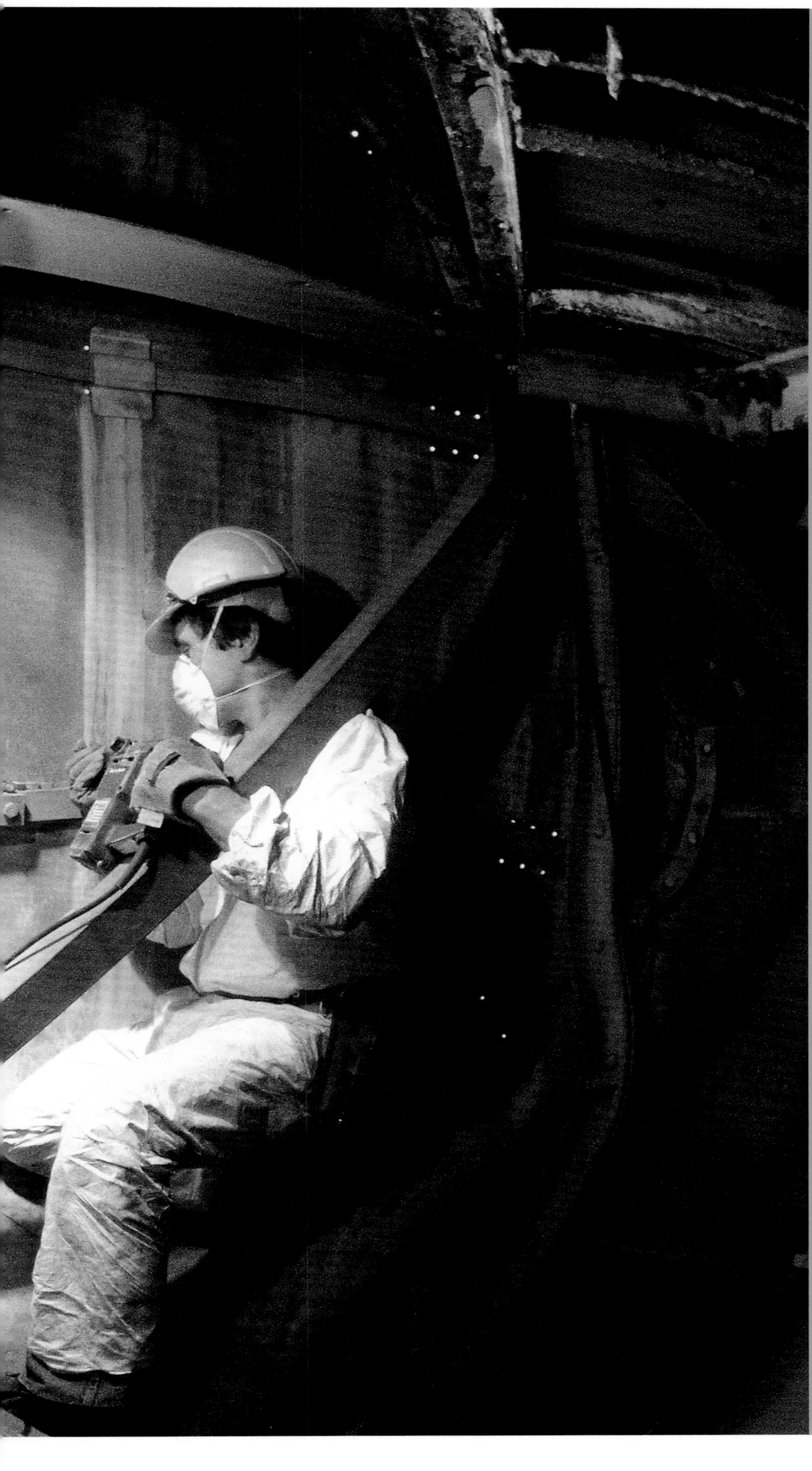

Eiffel's Design

Some 1800 armature bars—each one different in size and shape—form the vast interior strap-work that supports the Statue's copper skin. Part of Eiffel's ingenious design, the armature allows the skin to expand or contract with a change in the weather. Ten thousand linear feet of armature and the saddles that hold the bars in position were replaced, along with 30,000 copper rivets. The entire job took 18 workers twelve months to complete, since they could only remove and copy a maximum of twelve pieces in any 24-hour period for fear of weakening the Statue's structure. Only ten of the original bars remain—in the Statue's right foot—as an example of the original iron structure.

LEFT *While the inside man drives a rivet into a saddle to secure an armature bar, the outside man, above, holds metal against the skin to keep the rivet from coming through.*

LEFT *The last armature piece set into place bears the names of workers who replaced the bars along with the date. Despite the men's pride in having been part of the project, NPS officials ordered it removed and the names ground off.* **BELOW** *Inside view of the Statue's left index finger before (top), and after (bottom) replacing the corroded armature bars and saddles.* **OPPOSITE** *A close-up view of the Statue's intricate armature.*

Guided by Laser

A laser beam running from the Statue's mezzanine to her shoulder, guides the installation of a new emergency elevator. The lift gives Park Rangers easy access to visitors in distress on the stairs. A hydraulic elevator —one of the world's tallest—was also constructed to ferry passengers between the monument's lobby and the top of the pedestal. Workers drilled through 17 feet of solid concrete to insert the 90-foot shaft below ground.

Take the inside of the Statue, for example. Over the years she had been sealed with paint—seven layers in all—and two or three coatings of coal tar. The trick was to remove all of it without damaging the copper underneath. We also had to be careful that stirring up all that stuff didn't cause an explosion. We experimented with all kinds of chemicals. Finally we settled on liquid nitrogen cooled to –325° F, which made the paint flake off.

The tar proved more difficult. We tried everything for an abrasive. We even blasted samples with crushed walnut shells and ground cornhusks. Nothing worked until someone got the idea of using old-fashioned bicarbonate of soda. Yes, the kind that settles the stomach! We bombarded the inside of the Statue with 40 tons of Arm & Hammer baking soda, and by the time we were finished, you could see the original hammer marks on the copper.

Everyone agrees—Gustave Eiffel was a genius. When Bartholdi couldn't figure out how to support his colossal statue, he turned to the man who would one day forever change the landscape of Paris with his giant tower.

Eiffel was an engineer. He came up with the idea of supporting the Statue's copper skin by hanging it on iron straps called armature bars that were attached to a central pylon. All in all, some 1800 pieces of armature—each one different—made up this internal structure. Over the years, the armature became corroded and needed to be replaced. There was only one trick. No more than twelve of these bars could be removed at the same time. And each of the twelve had to be taken from a different spot.

When all was said and done, we replaced ten thousand linear feet of armature, weighing 35,000 pounds, with non-corrosive stainless steel. In fact, only ten of the original bars remain—in the right foot. They were left behind as an example of the original iron structure.

Each new phase of the project brought new problems—or as someone said, new challenges. Once the scaffolding was up, we were in a better position to

continued on page 150

OPPOSITE ABOVE *A National Elevator worker welds the hydraulic tube for the new passenger lift.* **OPPOSITE BOTTOM** *Alimark Company, contractor for the emergency elevator, installs railing for the tiny, two-person cab.* **FOLLOWING PAGES** *Wielding a cutting torch, an iron worker removes old steel in the crown room.* **INSET** *Local 40 Structural Ironworkers pin.*

RIGHT *A worker cuts away part of the familiar old helical stairway, inset. The revamped stairs feature wider railings and new steel rest platforms.*

ABOVE *A UBS crew examines the spike nearest the Statue's upraised arm before it's removed.* **RIGHT** *Slightly repositioned when the monument was erected in New York, the ray had, over the years, rubbed a hole in the arm as the Statue shifted with changes in wind and temperature.* **BELOW** *A French worker draws plans for repositioning the ray whose worn tip is seen on the sawhorse.*

PAGES 148-149 *As fog rolls in, workers install a refurbished ray in Liberty's crown.*
INSET *View from scaffolding surrounding Liberty's upraised arm.*

examine every inch of the monument from the outside.

One of the things about the Statue that never ceases to amaze me is how thin-skinned she is—less than the thickness of two pennies! Despite this, not even one percent of her copper had to be replaced. All in all, she had a few holes in the tip of her nose, in several curls and her right eye. Not bad for a 100-year-old lady. So we did a little cosmetic surgery and patched in new metal, then applied a few chemicals to turn the shiny copper green. She was as good as new.

On the island, work never stopped. By now, the press was covering us on almost a daily basis, and visitors jammed the gallery of our workshop to watch the progress. Part of selling the restoration to the public was enlisting the help of grassroots organizations.

Three hundred national organizations supported our drive. We got commitments of millions of dollars from people like the Disabled Vets of America, the Elks, the Masons, the DAR, and the Telephone Pioneers of America. An organization of the Bell System, the Pioneers held a bake sale. They raised $240,000. That's a lot of cupcakes. Then they held a giant bake-off and another $425,000 came in.

Just as important were the local campaigns—the Boy and Girl Scout troops, the Rotary Clubs, the Kiwanis, the churches and others that collected money. After a while, everybody wanted to get in on the act.

One man rode a motorized surfboard 3,000 miles to raise money. Another trekked across the country on foot, collecting contributions as he went. We even heard from the Hell's Angels! They donated $2,000.

During our four-year campaign, I met thousands of contributors. Maybe they only gave a few dollars, maybe more, but the sentiment was always the same: It was a way of saying thank you to America for freedoms offered and promises kept.

OPPOSITE *After a hard day's work, crew from Lehrer/McGovern ride the elevator down. The New York-based firm served as construction manager for the project, both hiring and overseeing contractors and suppliers with National Park Service and Foundation approval.*

McGOVERN

Chapter 6

KAUAI
OAHU
MOLOKAI
LANAI
KAHOOLAWE

Exterior Restoration

People always ask me how involved I got in the restoration. My answer—"Very!"

While I didn't always make it out to the island each time I visited New York, I always tried to meet with Briganti, May and one or two of the others, to check up on our progress. By now my name was being used in direct-mail pieces that blanketed the country, and I wanted to keep close tabs on all those dollars raised.

Much to my surprise, people really did read those long letters we sent out. When the return envelope came back, most of it was addressed to my attention. One of my favorite stories is Mary Miller.

Mary got one of my pitch letters and promptly wrote a check for $1000. Of course, we sent her a nice thank-you note, "signed" by me. I'm pretty sure she liked what I said, because she sent in another check—this one for $50,000.

continued on page 161

PRECEDING PAGES *Young visitors from a Roosevelt Island school peer in a window of the workshop on Liberty Island. In the foreground are wooden tools used to fashion the new torch.* **OPPOSITE** *With plastic sheeting protecting the Statue's face, workers make a rubber mold of the damaged nose.* **ABOVE LEFT** *Richard Knorr repairs a hole in the plaster nose that was made from the rubber mold.* **ABOVE RIGHT** *Coffee break on high.*

OPPOSITE *Exterior damage included a hole in the tip of the right curl.* **LEFT** *Workers remove the piece, which was shipped to Fiebiger's shop for repair.* **ABOVE** *A brief respite from the difficult task of removing the curl's rivets.* **BELOW** *Bruno Ranieri lifts the finished curl from its mold as Joe Fiebiger, at left, and NPS architect John Robbins look on.*

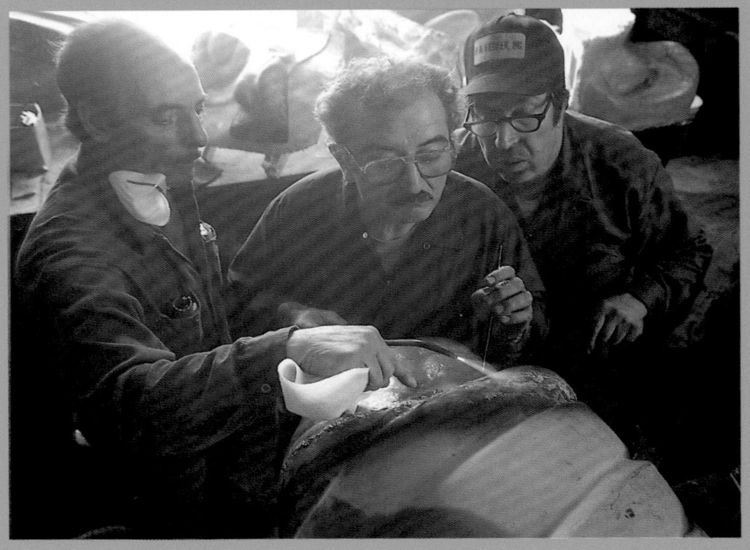

Replacing With the New

Despite the thinness of her copper—less than the thickness of two pennies—fewer than one percent of the Statue's copper had to be repaired or replaced. Holes in the tip of her nose, in several curls, and cracks in both eyes required special patchwork. All new copper was chemically treated to give it the same protective patina of the Statue that was naturally acquired over the years.

TOP *Workers cut away the damaged part of the curl.* **MIDDLE** *Re-affixed to the Statue, the curl with its new tip.* **BOTTOM** *Connie Bassett, the "patina lady," applies a special acid that will turn the new copper, green. The year 1986 was stamped into the new piece so workers in the future would know what was replaced.*

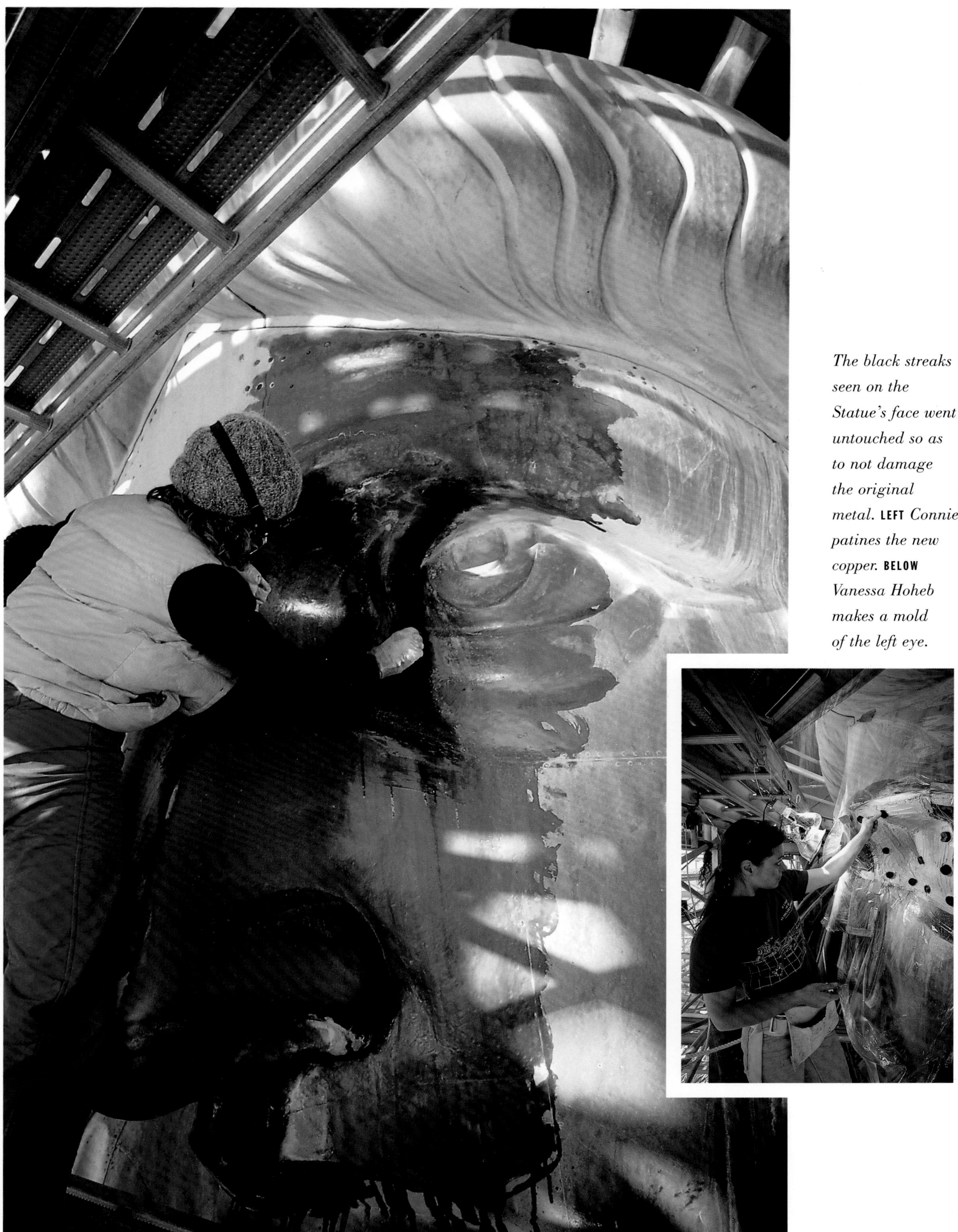

The black streaks seen on the Statue's face went untouched so as to not damage the original metal. **LEFT** *Connie patines the new copper.* **BELOW** *Vanessa Hoheb makes a mold of the left eye.*

P.A. FIEBIGER
Inc.
FIEBIGER INC

When I heard this, I thought I'd better call this time, and not write. I guess we connected over the phone because she mailed me another envelope.

It contained three checks—one for $25,000, one for $50,000 and one for $75,000. I used to wonder what she'd have given, if I'd sent her flowers! I was so grateful for her gift that I wanted to take her over to the Statue, but she was always busy. The last time she turned me down, she was doing her spring housecleaning. Imagine, an 87-year-old woman with a schedule tighter than mine.

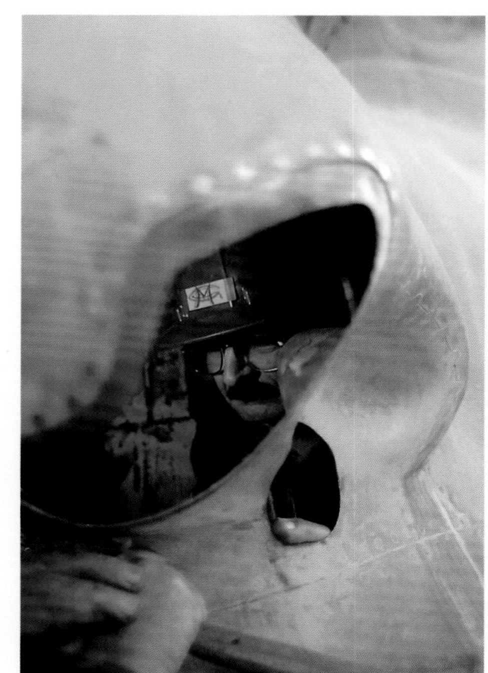

Work on the whole project was, in part, a joint effort between the French and the United States. Artisans from Reims, France built the new flame, then a Parisian firm covered it with gold leaf. Our workers from a few of the local unions weren't too happy about this, but they reluctantly went along in the interest of international relations.

Some of our most enthusiastic guests on the island were kids. They certainly were the most fun. School groups, scout troops, 4-H clubs, you name it. They came from all over, usually carrying a sack of money they had collected from bake sales, car washes and other moneymaking schemes. The rangers at the Statue were very nice and always tried to make a little ceremony out of the presentation.

Throughout the campaign, young people were one of our most important constituencies. I got hundreds of letters each week, many from schools. A lot of them included crayon drawings of the Statue, or essays about the Statue in 25 words or less, or poems in her honor, from budding Emma Lazaruses. One thing's for sure, most of these letters contained coins—frequently sent in a piggy bank!

continued on page 169

OPPOSITE *Joe Fiebiger helps install the new copper tip to the Statue's nose, while a worker rivets from inside, above.*

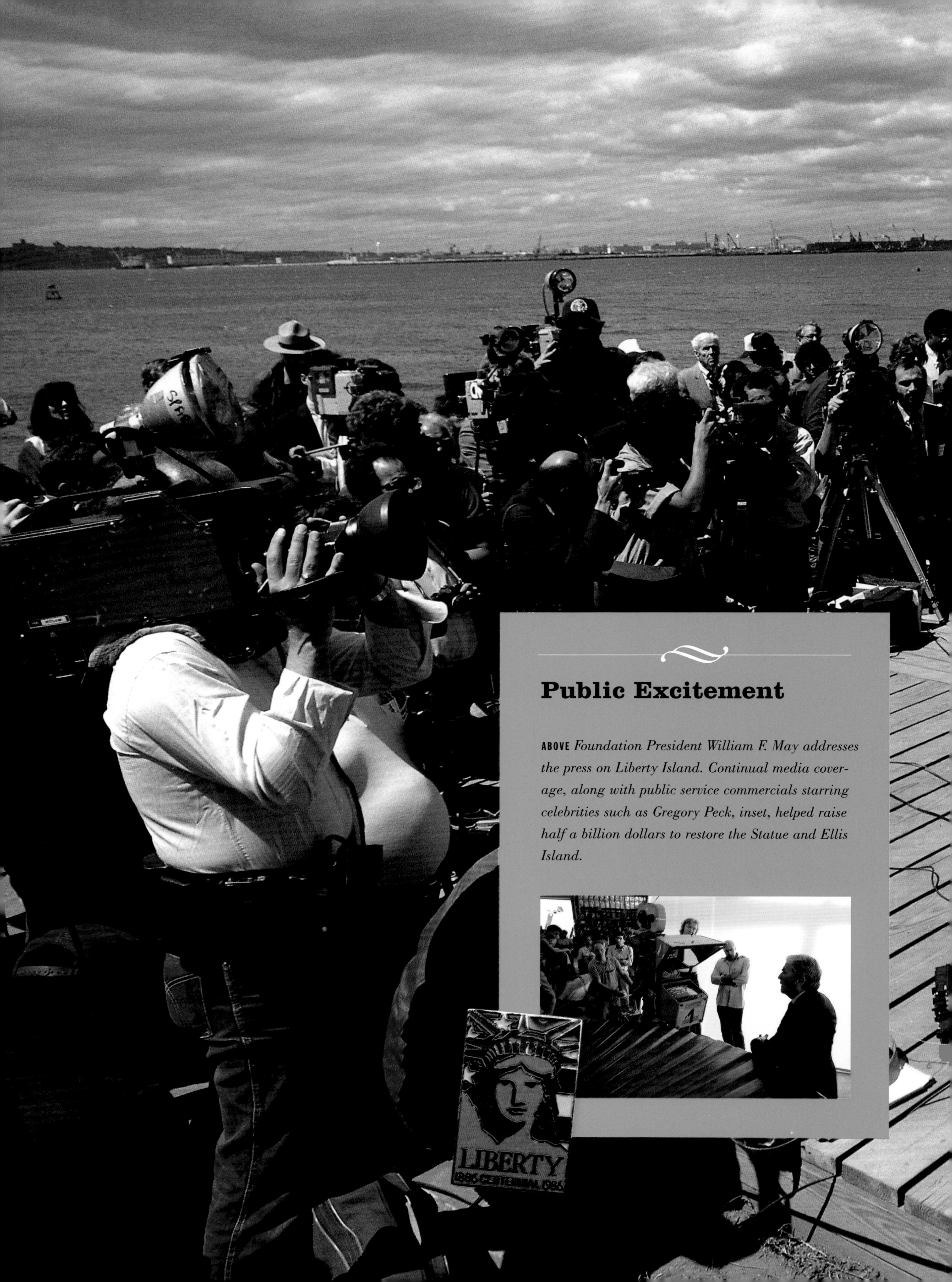

Public Excitement

ABOVE *Foundation President William F. May addresses the press on Liberty Island. Continual media coverage, along with public service commercials starring celebrities such as Gregory Peck, inset, helped raise half a billion dollars to restore the Statue and Ellis Island.*

WHN
WCBS 88
AP

TOP *Thierry Despont, architect for the torch, making a clay model of the new flame shortly after the scaffolding was completed. In the background the old torch, now on display in the Statue's museum.* **LEFT** *Additional models of the flame.* **BELOW** *French craftsmen take measurements to build a full-scale plaster reproduction of the flame in the workshop on Liberty Island.*

The architects decided to replicate the original flame with the ancient method of repoussé used to fabricate the Statue originally. A search for artisans skilled in the craft ended in Reims, France with ten men from the firm of Les Metalliers Champenois. **TOP** *After making the flame's plaster mold, a worker welds steel plates which have been heated and shaped to the plaster.* **LEFT** *Workers attach supports before smoothing concrete over the brackets, above, to strengthen the mold.*

Sections of the flame's mold are scattered on the workshop floor. Giant hooks on each piece enabled the heavy molds to be lifted by a crane.

A French worker first places a piece of copper inside a mold, then heats the metal with a torch before pounding it into shape with a mallet.

Armature bars for the flame conform to the plaster model. The new upper torch and flame, along with some of the larger armature pieces, were fashioned in the island workshop. A daily photographic record was kept by Peter. B. Kaplan, who outfitted the building with strobe lights lent to the project by Tekno. A number of other companies also assisted the Foundation and Kaplan with in-kind donations.

ABOVE *A French worker puts the last piece into the new flame. The black tube at right allowed him to communicate with the inside man, as the rivets are installed. Visiting artisan Kenneth Lynch reminisces with the French. While working on the monument in the 50s, Lynch found the original tools used to build the Statue. The instruments are now on display in the museum.*

Serge Pascal, a member of the French team, rivets a copper piece into place. Like his outside counterpart, he speaks via a black plastic hose.

All told, America's kids contributed $7 million dollars to the campaign—most of it in nickels, dimes and quarters. I felt sorry for the poor lady at the bank. We sent over so many coins covered with glue that she had to take them home to wash. They kept getting stuck in the change counter.

As work accelerated during the summer of '85, we had to close the island to the public. Some people in the government had a hard time with this decision. They didn't understand that with one year to go before the Statue reopened, we had a lot to do if we were to meet our deadline. Besides, the whole island was now a construction site.

We were ripping up walkways, digging trenches for new lighting, and overhauling the island's snack bar and gift shop. With all this activity, we couldn't afford to have the public get hurt and then turn around and sue us. Already our insurance bills were off the charts. Back then, it was difficult to sue the federal

continued on page 178

A Typical Day for the Metalworkers

RIGHT *A wooden mold holds hammered copper, which will become part of the railing for the new torch.*

BELOW *Jacque DuPont refines the lines on the decorative base of the torch. Despite a friendly rivalry between the French and the American union workers, both groups learned metalworking techniques from each other.*

BELOW *The pins of the American and French teams that worked on the new torch.*

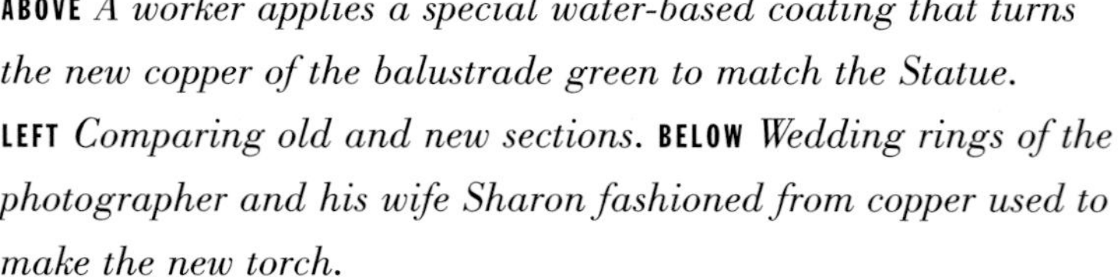

ABOVE *A worker applies a special water-based coating that turns the new copper of the balustrade green to match the Statue.* **LEFT** *Comparing old and new sections.* **BELOW** *Wedding rings of the photographer and his wife Sharon fashioned from copper used to make the new torch.*

PAGES 174-175 *Workers carry the underneath part of the torch's new balcony. Copper screening was placed over the air vents seen in the foreground, to prevent birds from entering the Statue.*

Philippe Poncet gives Lee Iacocca a first-hand look at the progress being made on the new balcony. Iacocca made frequent trips to the Statue to review its status. "I felt an obligation to the American people to make sure we brought the project in on time."

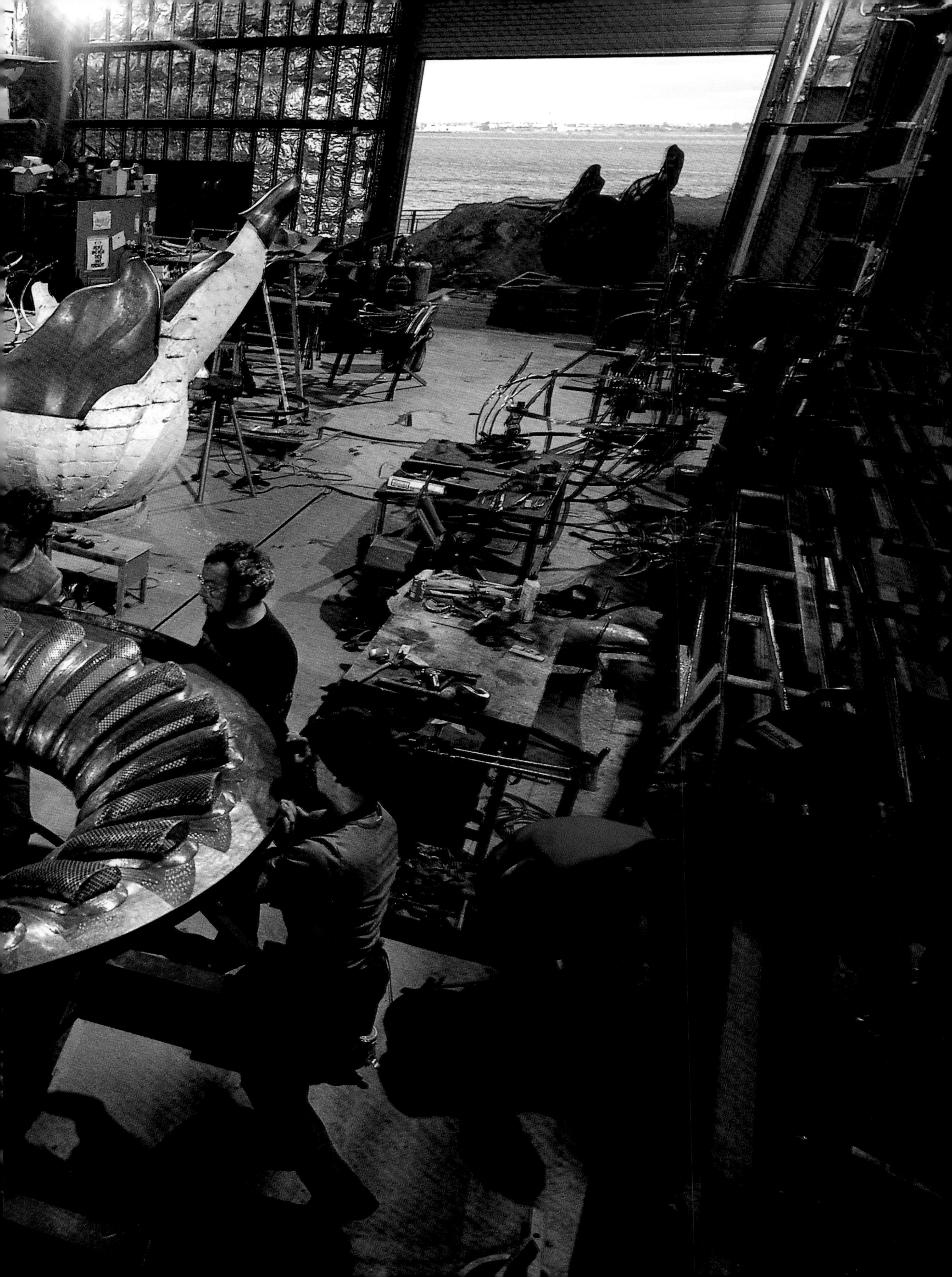

RIGHT *Robert Gohard and his son Fabrice, from Paris, France, carefully apply 15 oz. of gold leaf onto the new flame, a few inches at a time. The thin sheets, above, were 24K gold.*

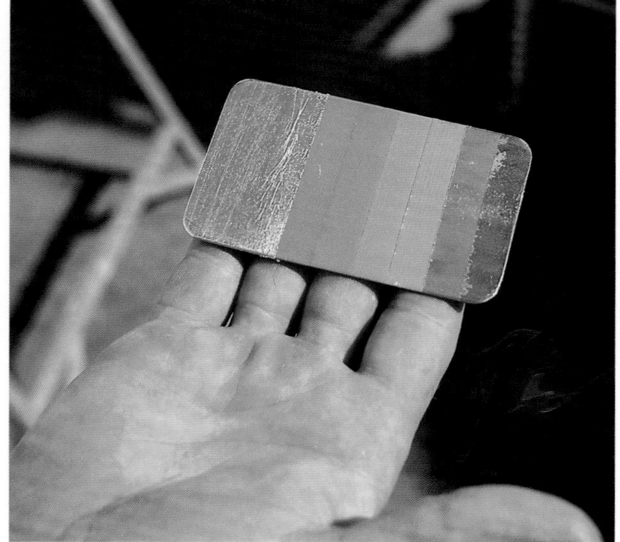

The gold leafing process included seven stages, demonstrated at left. First the copper was coated with an thin adhesive, above, after which sheets of gold leaf were applied with tweezers. The Gohards then brushed smooth the tissue-thin gold, before coating the layer with sealants.

government. You had to get their permission. But the Foundation was another story, and although some people didn't like it, we had to control access to the island. We couldn't afford not to.

As we entered the final year, our campaign accelerated. By now, thousands of news stories had appeared in print chronicling some aspect of the restoration. We also benefited from an Ad Council campaign—150 million dollars worth of free advertising in print and broadcast media. Every time an ad ran, it carried our address. Shortly afterwards, we'd see a surge in donations.

In the fall of '85, we hoisted the new torch aloft and reattached the crown's rays. We also began to dismantle the scaffolding. The restoration was entering its final phase.

That October, we also turned our attention to the Statue's hundredth birthday in 1986. Although her actual anniversary is October 28th, we decided to celebrate in July when the weather—if our luck held out—would be nicer. We dubbed our celebration "Liberty Weekend," to coincide with July 4th. It would be the biggest party New York had ever seen.

David Wolper came on board as producer. Fresh from staging the opening and closing ceremonies for the '84 Olympics, he would receive no salary, only expenses. Now of course, I had two projects to worry about. And to pay for.

OPPOSITE *An electrician mounts new lamps on the balcony.* **FOLLOWING PAGES** *Jay Lippert, left, Bob Panko, head of security, and Tally stand watch over the Statue's new torch, the night before it was re-attached to the Statue. Bomb threats prompted the heightened vigilance.*

EXIT
PLEASE
DO NOT TOUCH
THE PATINA

Chapter 7

Final Touches

A funny thing happened on the way to the Statue's completion—I got fired.

It happened on a Friday night in February 1986. I received a telegram from Secretary of the Interior Donald Hodel. On the one hand, it praised me for my past efforts, and then went on to say that because there's a "potential of future conflict or the appearance thereof" between my roles as chairman of the Centennial Commission and the Statue of Liberty-Ellis Island Foundation, I had to leave the commission. Trying to interpret all this Washington doublespeak, I think they were saying I couldn't raise the money and then recommend how to spend it.

None of this made sense. Obviously Washington has never heard of accountability. From the very beginning, I wanted to make sure that the money we raised was spent wisely. And as I got more involved, this became even more important to me.

After all, the kids who sent in their hard-earned nickels and dimes sent them to me—not to the Secretary of the Interior. I felt an obligation to do right by them. It's the way I was brought up.

continued on page 190

PRECEDING PAGES *The new flame attached to the Statue. Specially designed illumination makes the torch visible for miles.*
OPPOSITE *As the exterior restoration drew to a close, workers began removing the scaffolding.*

ABOVE *Bird's eye view of the new flame being hoisted into place in November of 1985. A remote camera, mounted on the cable as seen on the opposite page—about one inch from the top of the photograph—captured this rare view.*

UBS

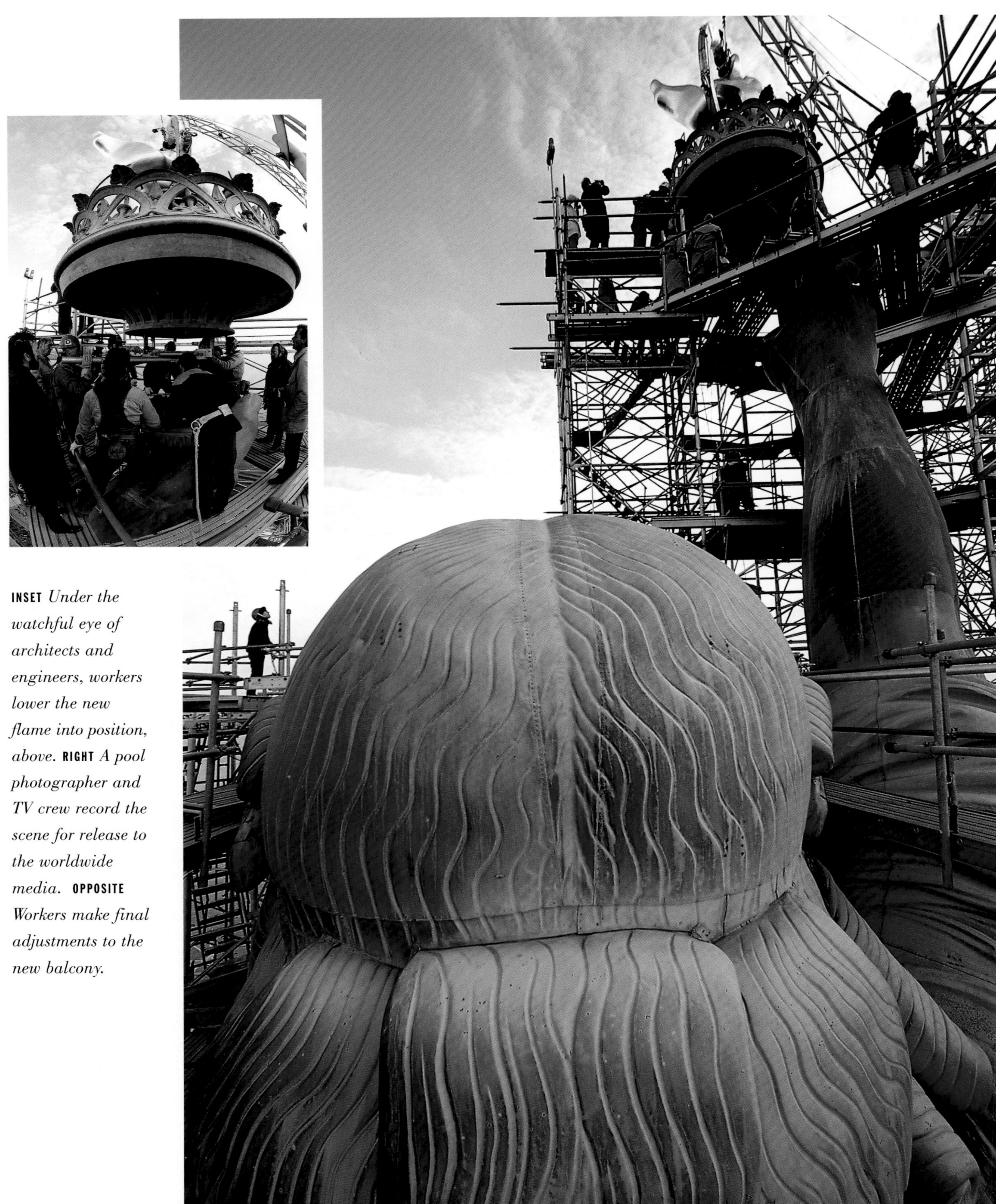

INSET *Under the watchful eye of architects and engineers, workers lower the new flame into position, above.* **RIGHT** *A pool photographer and TV crew record the scene for release to the worldwide media.* **OPPOSITE** *Workers make final adjustments to the new balcony.*

Speaking of upbringing, when my mother heard I got canned, she called me and wanted to know what happened? She was very protective and, like a good Italian mother, very defensive of her only son. "What's wrong? You were doing so well. What would have happened if you were doing poorly?" I honestly couldn't answer her.

Initially I was angry—my blood pressure shot up a few points—but I was determined to finish the project—politics or no politics.

The restoration proceeded on schedule. By April 1986, the scaffolding was down and the world caught a sneak preview of the new torch. But we were still far from finished. And the clock was ticking.

All along, it was our intention to place the old torch inside the main entrance to the Statue. That was easier said than done. We ended up having to chip away the stones surrounding the front door, then digging a trench to get it inside.

The museum itself was a great idea. It tells not only the history of the Statue, but also how she was built. And much to the delight of kids everywhere, it includes two life-size replicas of the Statue's face and foot.

Once the ceremonies for Liberty Weekend were finalized, we began rounding up celebrities to perform at the festivities. It seemed as though everyone we asked responded enthusiastically including Frank Sinatra, Itzhak Perlman, Zubin Mehta and the New York Philharmonic, Willie Nelson, Elizabeth Taylor, Liza Minnelli, to name but a few. They all gave of their time and talent and in no small measure helped make the celebration very special.

continued on page 198

The campaign to save the Lady captured the imagination of America's children, much as building the Statue inspired their counterparts 100 years ago. Fifteen million young people raised $7 million for the restoration—most of it in nickels, dimes and quarters. **ABOVE** *Making a fundraising commercial.* **OPPOSITE** *"Liberty" Maypole at a school in Queens, New York.*

Americans from all walks of life pitched in to help save the Statue including unions, fraternal organizations and community groups. Each had their own campaign button similar to the ones above.

LEFT *Mail arrived daily at the Foundation. Some letters contained a check; others, a note or picture including the image of the Statue made from coins and dollar bills, above left.* **ABOVE** *The Disabled Veterans of American donated $1 million.* **RIGHT** *A Statue float in the Macy's Thanksgiving Day Parade followed by the old torch, pages 194-195, helped publicize the restoration on national television. Photo by Bob Di Jacomo © Peter B. Kaplan 1984, NYC*

1460

SONY
MIDORI
MELON
LIQUEUR
Enjoy
Coca-Cola
10:27
COME AND MEET
THOSE DANCING FEET
42ND STREET
BURGER KING
OPEN

JVC
AUDIO
Pizza
the LIGHT of LIBERTY

Lee Iacocca holds one of three special coins issued by the U.S. Mint to honor the Statue. Sale of the commemoratives raised $75 million.

Taking a page from the original fund-raising campaign to build the Statue, the Foundation licensed a number of products, many of which featured the Statue's image. A portion of each sale helped pay for the restoration. At left, a flashing light pin.

Each of the licensed products bore the Foundation's official logo. Several hundred items were officially sponsored ranging from Tiffany watches to charcoal briquettes, above, and kites, below.

LEFT *High-speed machines stitch the Statue's image on jackets designed especially for the 100th anniversary celebration.*

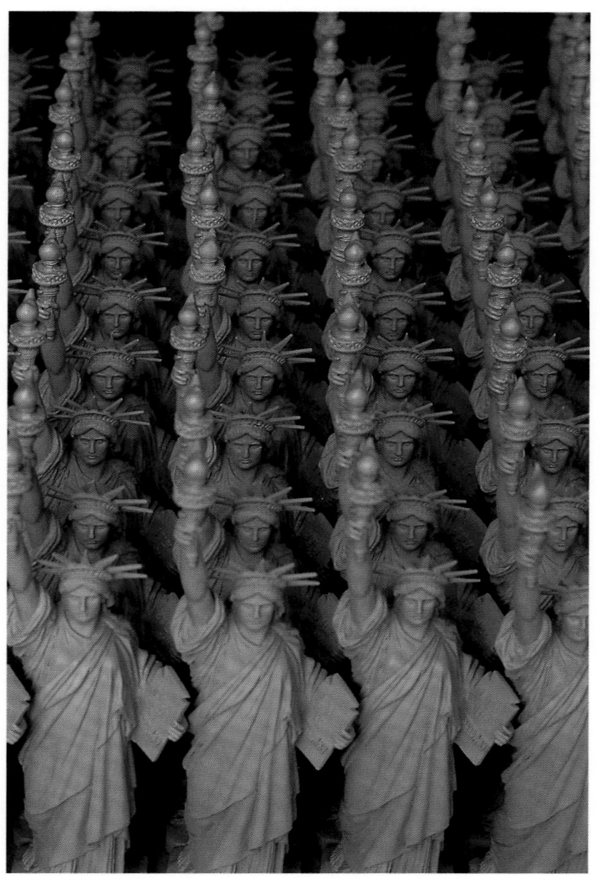

At the Barrett Colea factory on Long Island, a worker sprays hundreds of resin statues with green paint to simulate Liberty's patina. After drying, the licensed souvenirs were attached to replicas of the pedestal, and then numbered. **RIGHT** *Among the novelties offered were food items such as pretzels. Licensed products generated seven million dollars for the restoration.*

At one point during the long planning process we decided that we'd have President Reagan present a Medal of Liberty to ten living Americans who were born overseas but made a contribution to American life.

We set up a selection committee—another blue-ribbon panel—that included such prominent people as Mario Cuomo, Ted Kennedy, Barbara Walters, Teddy White and Arthur Schlesinger, Jr. They all took their job seriously and each drew up a list of nominees.

When we met, we debated the merits of every name put forward. There were so many worthy candidates that we decided to increase the list from 10 to 12 as if that would help. In the end, we realized that although we had selected only twelve, they were really representative of the dozens who could have been honored.

As the big celebration drew closer, it seemed as if all New York caught Liberty fever. Everywhere you went there were souvenirs—and a little piece of history for sale.

Liberty pasta, jackets, t-shirts, earrings, shower curtains, cookies, spoons, bandanas, mugs and miniature statues—blanketed the city. Each manufacturer had asked the Foundation to grant a license for a particular product, which meant we'd get a piece of the action. We tried to be careful with the Lady's image, but every now and then we got some strange requests. A casket company wanted our endorsement, along with a manufacturer of toilet paper, but we said no. We had our standards.

Liberty Weekend spanned four days, but the Statue's big moment came on the night of July 3rd. Honored guests including President François Mitterand of

continued on page 216

ABOVE *Tickets to a concert at the Kennedy Center in Washington, D.C. on October 28, 1985. The event kicked off a year-long celebration of the Statue's Centennial.* **OPPOSITE** *Under a gray December sky, a worker dismantles the scaffolding.*

Working at the top

For dozens of construction workers on the Statue project, climbing about scaffolding reaching 300 feet into the air was all part of a day's work. Like their counterparts of yesteryear who are seen perched on iron girders in historic photos of New York, the men exhibited no fear, something that constantly amazed photographer Peter B. Kaplan. "I always experienced an uneasiness as I started to move about the scaffold. At first I wore a safety belt, but then I realized it hampered me. A little bit of fear was always there but after a while it disappeared because the photographer in me took over. All I could think about was the next image, the next angle." Known for photographing objects from great heights, Kaplan regards his Statue coverage as his finest body of work. "It was my chance to be part of history, to capture images never seen before...and hopefully to pass them on to future generations."

Sitting on top of the world: Workers take a break from removing the scaffolding.

G.S.G.S.B.

OPPOSITE *Washing down the Statue.* **ABOVE** *Vietnam veterans, now construction workers, hold aloft a US flag that once flew over a captured hill in Southeast Asia.* **RIGHT** *Empty footlights allow painters a breath of fresh air.* **BELOW** *Taking a break.* **FOLLOWING PAGES** *The Statue at sunrise, before the old torch was removed.*

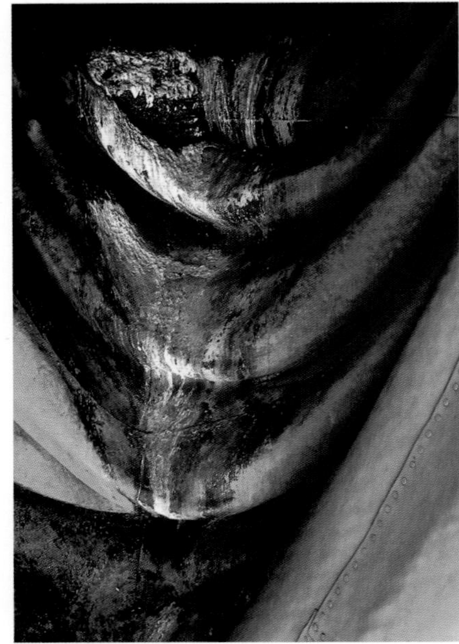

PRECEDING PAGES *For several years at sunrise, the photographer noticed a golden glistening in the Statue's left sleeve. When he was able to view the area up close the mystery was solved: seven layers of mud-swallow nests were found in the folds of the garment, seen in the top left photo.* **CENTER LEFT** *A grackle brings food back to its young fledglings, whose nest is buried deep under the ribbon on the Statue's right shoulder, below left.* **ABOVE** *Once a stopover for migrating Canadian geese, the monument during the restoration became home to a year-round flock. When the Statue reopened, the birds sought more secluded quarters on deserted sections of nearby Ellis Island.*

No longer home to mud-swallows, the sleeve now claims a pair of nesting peregrine falcons.

Camera Obscura

While photographing the inside of the Statue's left arm, photographer Peter B. Kaplan discovered a small drain hole in the monument that made the enclosure a natural camera obscura. As light rays streamed through the hole on one wall of the arm, an image of the outside surroundings was projected upside down on another wall. Thought to date back as far as the 5th century BC, this ancient method of viewing an image by projecting light into a dark enclosure was a precursor to the modern camera.

BELOW *Peter B. Kaplan readies his camera to photograph the projection seen in the large photo at right. When sunlight poured through a tiny hole in a piece of foil placed over the drain—seen in the bottom right of the photograph below—the outline of the Statue's observation deck and star-shaped base appeared on the wall of the arm. Kaplan used the foil to make the drain hole smaller, which then sharpened the image. The large stainless steel bar seen in the photo is part of the Statue's internal support system.*

Photo by David Wills © Peter B. Kaplan 1983

INSET *Outside view of the Statue that was projected on the wall of the left arm shows the base and the observation deck of the monument's pedestal.*

In addition to work on the Statue itself, the entire Liberty Island underwent a facelift. Landscaping, upgrading of utilities and a renovated snack bar and gift shop were included in the project. **ABOVE** *Surveying the entrance promenade.*

BELOW *Sifting through the rubble, a worker uncovers arrowheads and oyster shells on the twelve-acre island, once fishing grounds for the native Americans who lived in the area.*

TOP *Proudly displaying its participation in the restoration, General Electric supplied the new lighting for the renovated Statue.* **LEFT** *A makeshift calendar marked off the remaining days before the Statue reopened to the public.* **RIGHT** *Holding their own: Foundation Project Director Larry Bellante of GSGSB, a Pennsylvania-based architectural and engineering firm, emphatically makes a point to Deputy Superintendent Kevin Buckley, while Manny Strumpf, public information officer for the Park Service looks on. Despite occasional disagreements, the public-private project was delivered on schedule.*

ABOVE *Architects and consultants test new lighting on a miniature model in the workshop.* **LEFT** *Workers pour concrete into one of five pits that will hold new lighting for the Statue.*

ABOVE *Urban Foundation Company pin. Urban supplied the concrete for the project.* **INSET** *Lighting designer Howard Brandston, left, checks the angle of the spotlights.*

ABOVE RIGHT *Foremen check drawings for the Statue's new interior, which includes a 7,000 square-foot museum.* **RIGHT** *A jackhammer-wielding worker chips away at the Statue's original concrete foundation, to make way for new interior construction.*

The Statue's original balcony slowly makes its way back to the monument, where it will become the centerpiece of the new museum. **OPPOSITE** *A tight fit necessitated widening the entrance by removing stones from the doorway.* **BELOW** *Pin from a local union.*

LEHRER

France gathered at Governors Island to watch Ronald Reagan re-light the Statue. The President activated a laser beam that shot across the water, setting off a light show that gradually revealed the "new" Statue, from her base to her crown. Then came the grand finale. Reagan threw a switch and the new torch beamed with brilliance. In the background a hundred-piece orchestra and five-hundred voice choir performed "America the Beautiful". I was never more moved. If you didn't get goose bumps then, you had to be dead.

Earlier that evening, on near-by Ellis Island, Chief Justice of the United States Warren Burger had administered the oath of citizenship to 500 immigrants, a reminder that our country is a nation made up of people from other lands.

On Friday, July 4th, there was a massive traffic jam in the Harbor as 40,000 boats jockeyed for position to watch the parade of Tall Ships. The vessels were every size and shape imaginable. I swear you could cross from one shore to the other by hopping from boat to boat. Later that night we witnessed one of the largest fireworks displays the world has ever seen. I ought to know. We paid two million bucks for the explosives.

On Saturday, there was a free concert on the Great Lawn in Central Park. Eight hundred thousand people attended. Most had come early to picnic and get a good spot, but with that many people you had to arrive before dawn!

The final bash came on Sunday at Giants Stadium in New Jersey. Fifty thousand people partied for three hours as we paid tribute to all the laborers who worked on the project.

Some 10 million people partied and spent money in New York that weekend. Best of all, not one crime was committed. Even thugs took a holiday. But it wasn't just the city that celebrated. For the country, the weekend rekindled a spirit of patriotism not seen since the bicentennial.

All in all, it was one helluva party!

OPPOSITE ABOVE *Workers slide the balcony into position near the entrance to the Statue.* **OPPOSITE LEFT** *A worker cuts away at the concrete to run electrical wires.* **OPPOSITE RIGHT** *Excavation for the new museum.* **FOLLOWING PAGES** *Covered in protective plastic, the old torch awaits its unveiling when the Statue reopens in July of 1986.*

Chapter 8

Liberty Weekend

Of all the special moments during the four-year project, there is one that is sharply etched in my memory.

At one point, ABC Television decided to interview a number of people, including me, on what liberty means to them. As they wired me up, I listened to the satellite feed and heard Bishop Desmond Tutu speak from Johannesburg about the freedom he was fighting for but didn't have yet. And then I heard Anatoly Shcharansky talking from Jerusalem about his years in a Russian prison and the joy in his newfound freedom.

Then it was my turn. And I thought, what in the world do I have to offer? I've never been anything but free. Freedom was my birthright. Like so many others, I've always taken liberty for granted. I don't remember what I said that day. I only remember being moved listening to Shcharansky and Tutu. They were the experts on freedom. Not me!

It's been almost twenty years since we restored the Statue. And after all this time, I still don't know what liberty is—at least not the way these two gentlemen

continued on page 228

PRECEDING PAGES *With "bombs bursting in air"...the Statue celebrates its hundredth birthday during Liberty Weekend, a four-day extravaganza during July of 1986 that was viewed via satellite by one and a half billion people around the world.* **OPPOSITE** *Streaks of light from exploding fireworks frame the monument on July 4th. The photographer captured this view using a special fish-eye lens on his camera.*

© Laura Mueller Woods / Peter B. Kaplan Images LTD.

During the festivities, the entire city came to a standstill as millions of New Yorkers joined with out-of-towners to honor America's special Lady. Bathed in red, white and blue, the towering Empire State Building— after 9/11, New York's tallest structure. **INSET** *Ten tons of pyrotechnics explode over New York Harbor. At the time it was the largest fireworks display ever offered in the United States.*

© Norman O. Tomalin 1986 / Peter B. Kaplan Images, LTD.

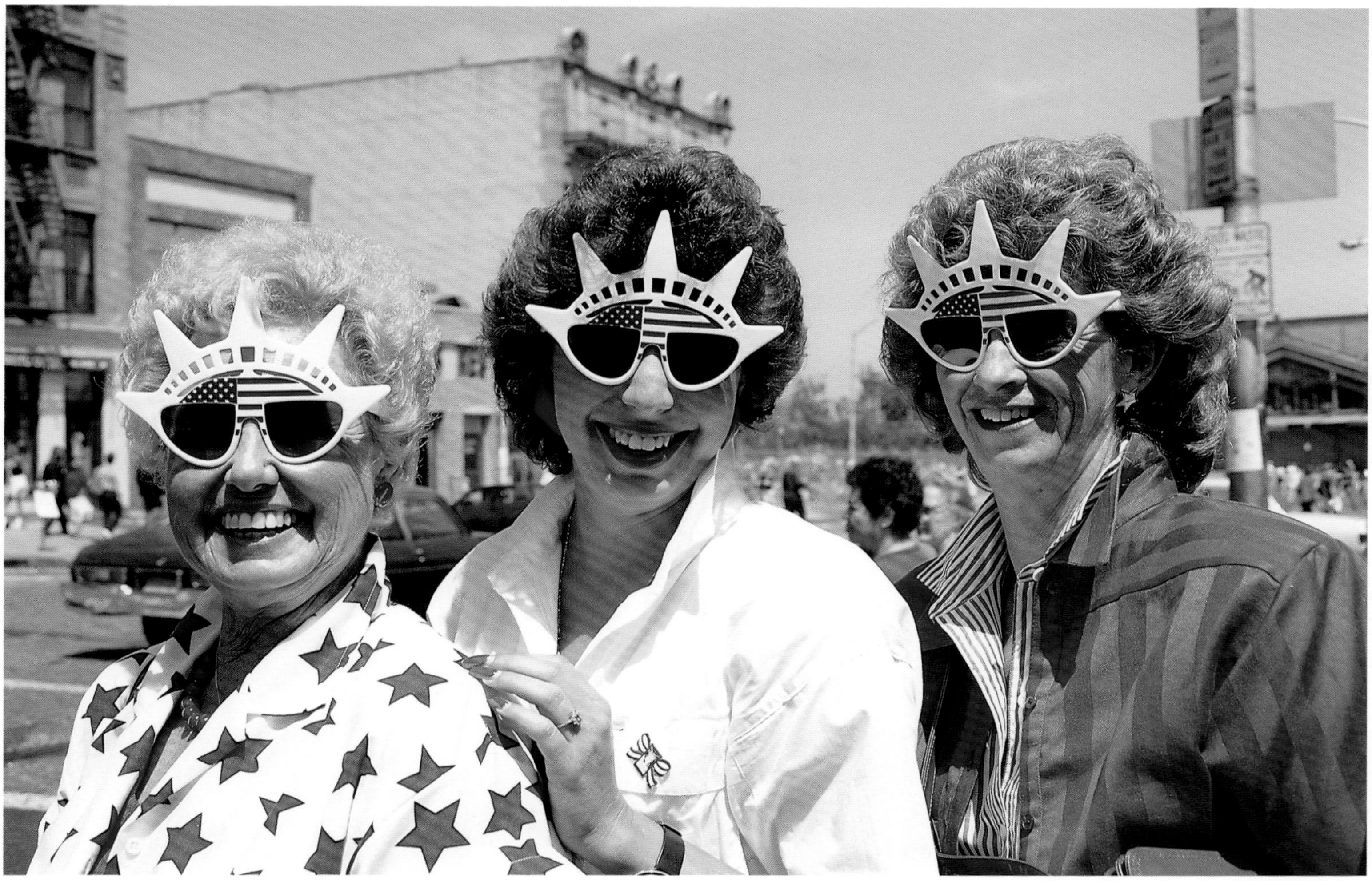

© Steven Borns 1986 / Peter B. Kaplan Images, LTD.

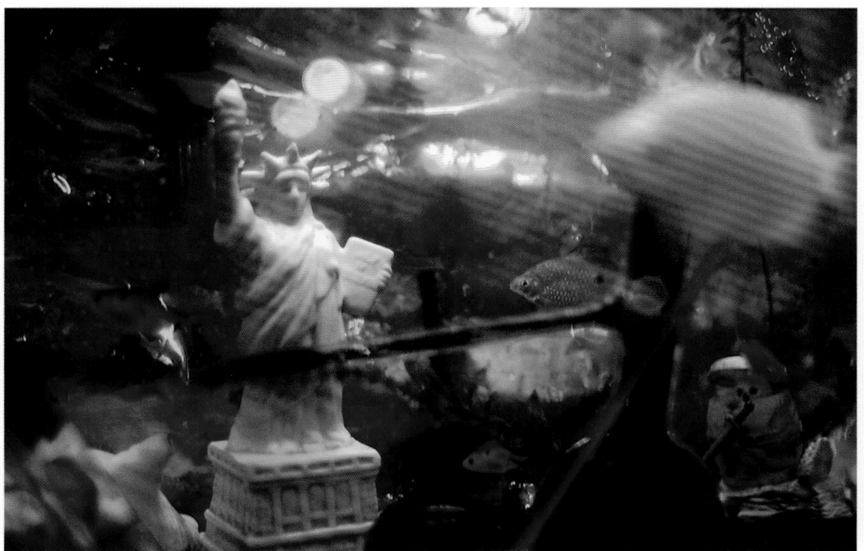

TOP *Liberty fever seized the city, with red, white and blue "de rigueur" of the day. Visitors donned Liberty glasses, crowns, and just about anything with a patriotic theme. Statue replicas abounded, some in the oddest of places: at the bottom of a fish tank in Chinatown, above; in front of a shop in the Village, at right.*

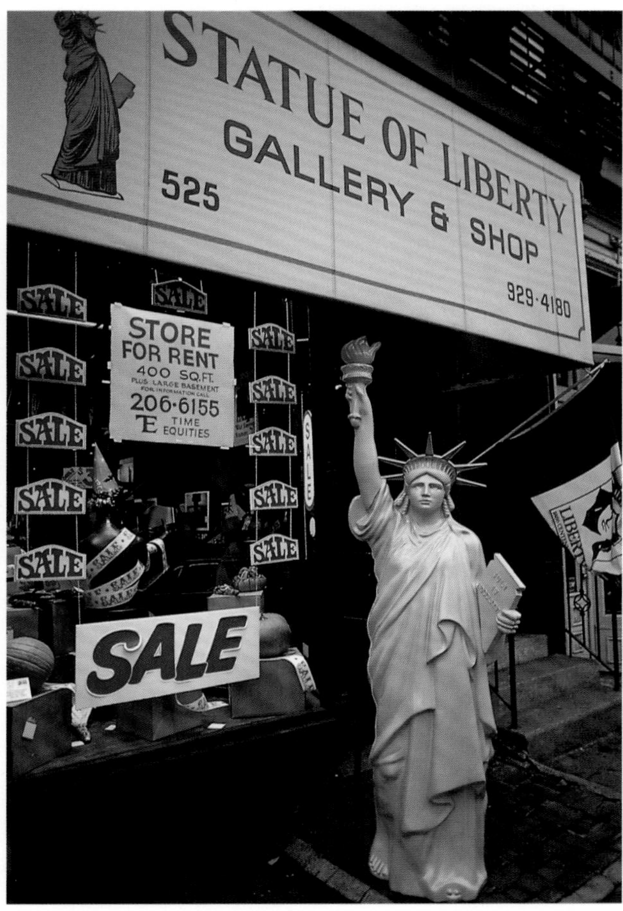

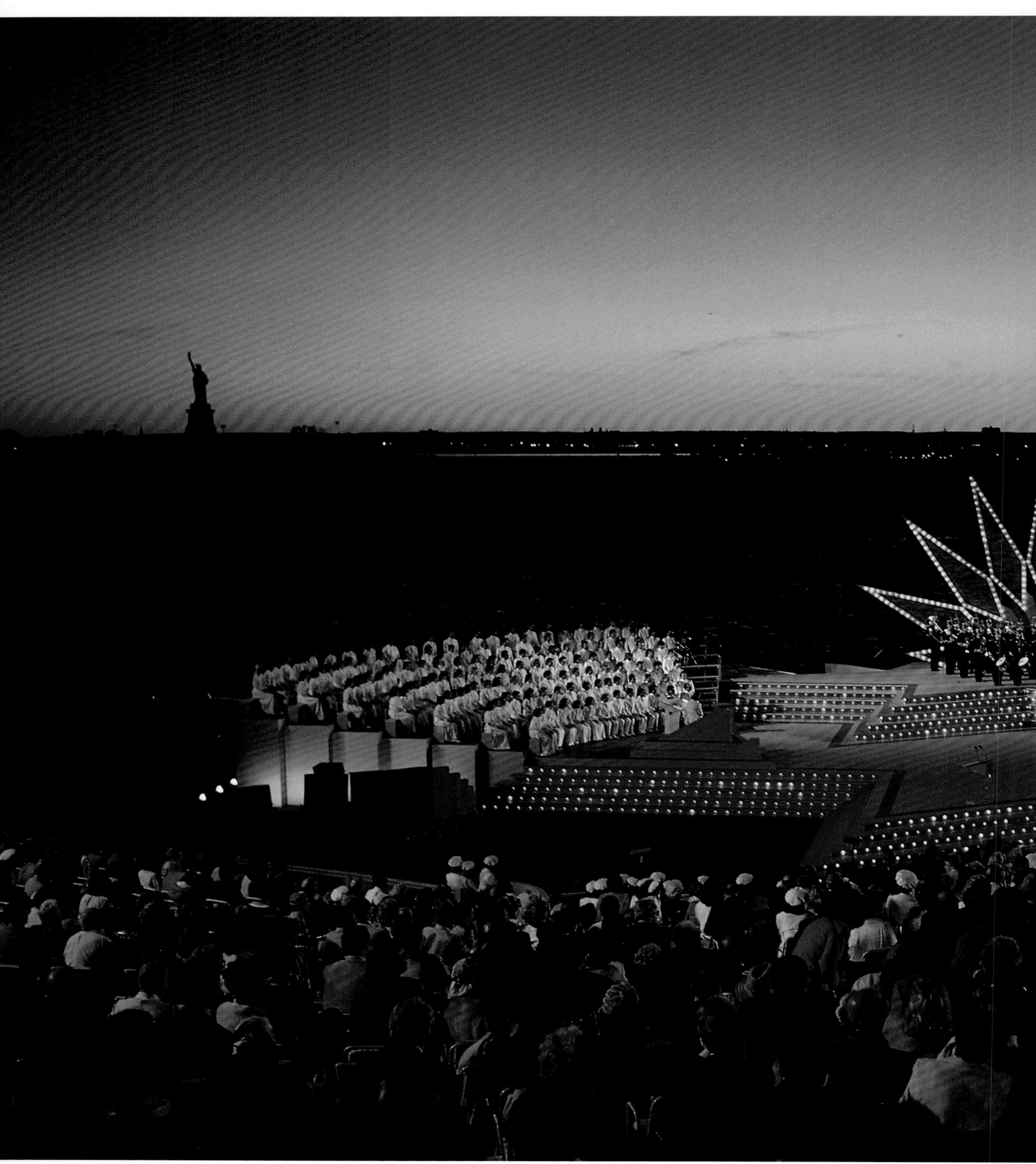

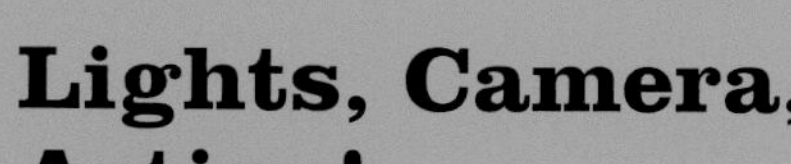

Lights, Camera, Action!

Opening ceremonies for Liberty Weekend took place on Governors Island in New York Harbor. Before an audience of 3,000 guests and 1,000 members of the international press corps, President Ronald Reagan and his French counterpart, François Mitterand, rededicated the Statue.

LEFT *With a darkened Liberty in the background, all eyes focus on the open-air stage and President Mitterand, bottom right. With the First Lady at his side, Ronald Reagan addresses the crowd before relighting the Statue.*

All 3 Photos © Declan Haun 1986 / Peter B. Kaplan Images, LTD.

did, or in the way the millions of immigrants who journeyed to America in search of freedom understand it. I do know one thing. I'm grateful for it, and after September 11, I cherish freedom more than ever. And I also know that it brings with it obligations—to pass this incredible gift on to our children and grandchildren.

As I look back on my life, helping to restore the Statue of Liberty is one of the best things I ever did. Time and time again during the four years I was involved, I thought of my father and those few times we visited the Statue.

continued on page 232

Signaled by a special laser beam activated by the President, a technician in a control booth at the Statue slowly lights the monument, beginning with the star-shaped foundation at top, then the pedestal, center, and finally ending with the Statue and new torch, bottom right.

Photo by J. Stephen Hall © Peter B. Kaplan 1986

Photo by J. Stephen Hall © Peter B. Kaplan 1986

Opening ceremonies featured a 100-piece orchestra, a 120-trumpet band, an original musical composition, and appearances by some of America's top entertainers. **LEFT AND INSET** *A performance of Neil Diamond's "Coming to America" highlights the immigrant experience and its connection to the Statue, now relit in the background.* **BELOW** *Elizabeth Taylor, an immigrant from England, at the ceremony.*

2 Photos © Barbara Bauman 1986 / Peter B. Kaplan Images, LTD.

Like so many immigrants—my father wanted to pass on his heritage. I realize now that part of him was intimately connected to the Statue. She welcomed him with open arms and the promise of a better life. All he had to do was work hard.

He kept his end of the bargain. She kept hers.

I've visited the Statue on several occasions since we celebrated her centennial. Once I brought my grown daughters, Kathi and Lia. Somehow, I felt a need to tell my father's story to them, and as we walked around the restored monument, I pointed out what we fixed and who gave what. I even threw in a little civics lesson about what the Statue represents. They smiled politely and wandered off. I hoped they'd get the message, as I did. And I hoped they'd pass it on to my grandkids.

If my father were still here, how proud he'd be—not just of the family he started and the success of his children, but that for a little while I was a caretaker of the Lady in the Harbor. She meant the world to him.

Now she means the same to me.

As part of the rededication, Warren Burger, above right, Chief Justice of the United States, administered the oath of citizenship to several hundred petitioners on near-by Ellis Island. Representing some 50 different countries, the applicants included the famous such as ballet dancer and choreographer Mikhail Baryshnikov, above left, as well as those known only to family and friends. **OPPOSITE** *Capping the opening ceremonies, a firework display from Ruggieri of France.* **INSET** *A new American beaming with pride.*

© Barbara Bauman 1986 / Peter B. Kaplan Images, LTD.

© Sam Garcia 1986 / Peter B. Kaplan Images, LTD.

Photo by Joel Gordon © Peter B. Kaplan 1986

July 4th brought day-long festivities including Op-Sail and a concert by the US Marine Corps Band, above. That night, a spectacular fireworks display lit up the Harbor. Op-Sail, one of the largest parades of sailing ships ever assembled, attracted vessels from some 30 nations. As the cortege, led by Sandy Hook pilots, made its way past the Statue, sailors climbed the ships' masts in a special salute to the Lady.

© Laura Mueller Woods / Peter B. Kaplan 1986

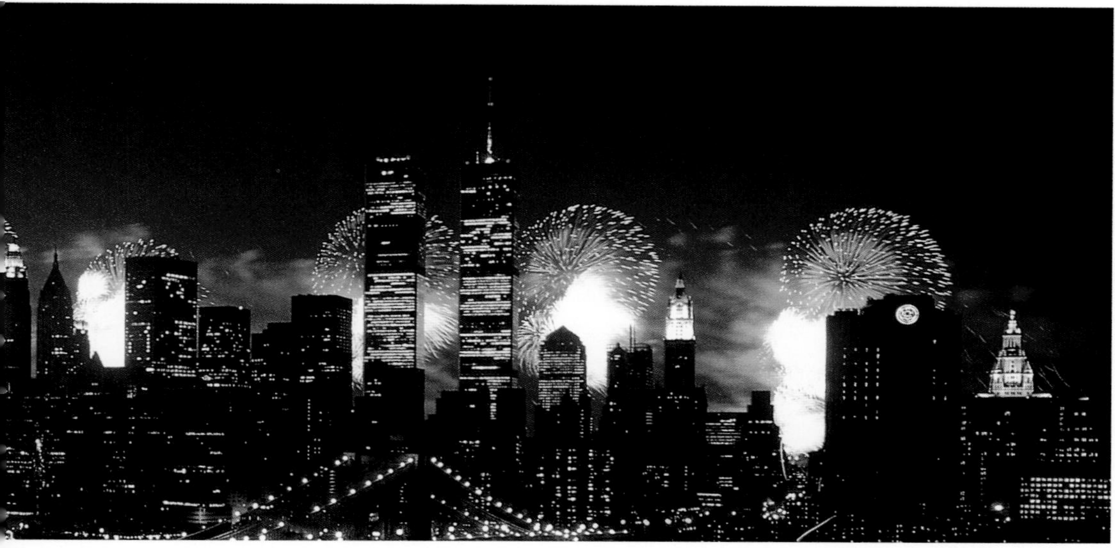

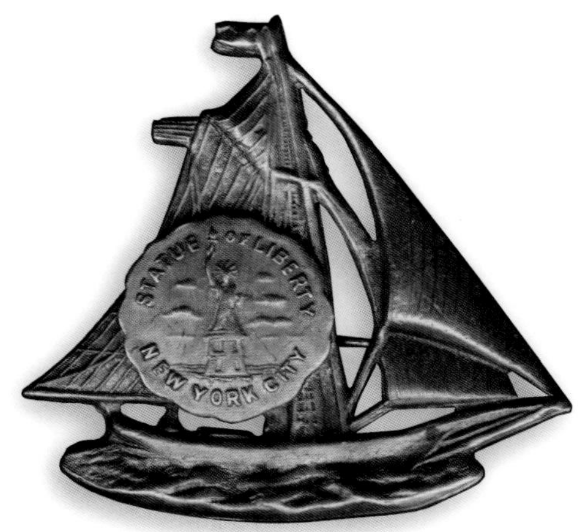

LEFT *Ten tons of fireworks detonate from forty-one barges that ring lower Manhattan.* **ABOVE** *An early Statue pin dating back to the 1940s.*

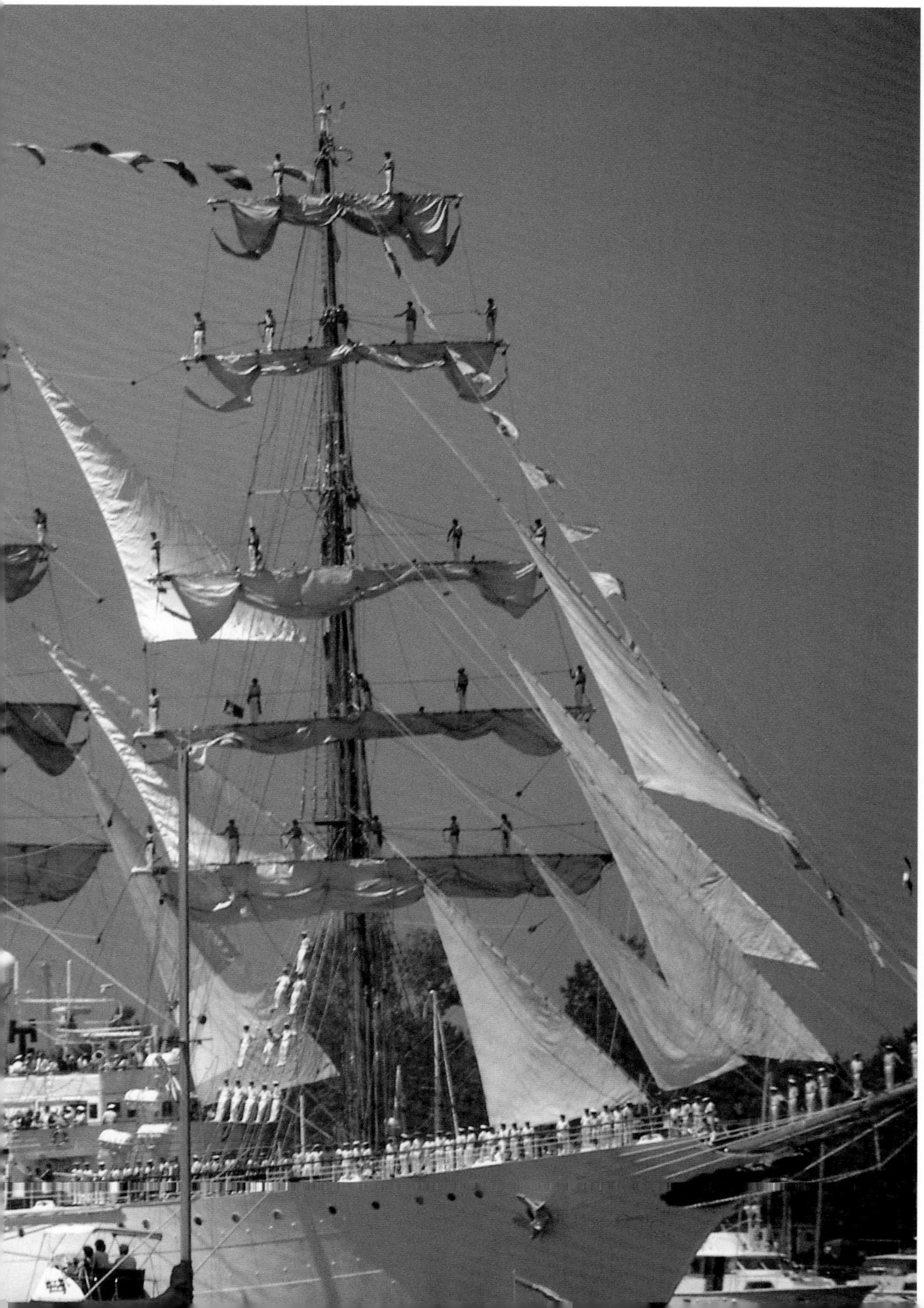

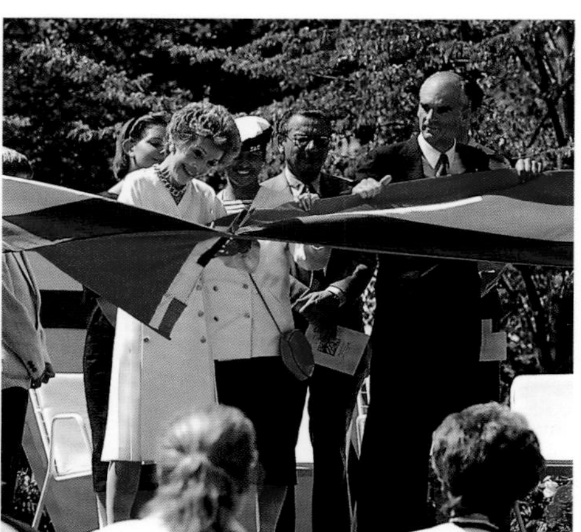

ABOVE *First Lady Nancy Reagan, with the aid of Secretary of the Interior Donald Hodel, cuts the ribbon reopening the Statue on July 5th. Closed to the public since mid-1985, the monument attracted thousands of tourists opening day, below.*

© Steven Borns 1986 / Peter B. Kaplan Images, LTD.

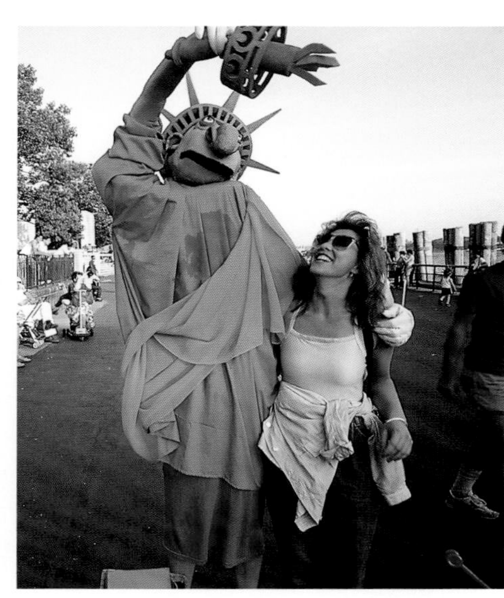

TOP *"New York threw one heck of a party" proclaimed one newspaper as millions jammed the streets to participate in the festivities. For some, the highlight was a visit to the Statue, where the old torch, at right, and a life-size model of the Statue's right foot, above, were main attractions.* **PAGES 236-237** *An outdoor concert in Central Park on July 5th attracted 800,000 people. Many came early to picnic and claim a space for the performance, which included the New York Philharmonic.*

© Declan Haun 1986 / Peter B. Kaplan Images, LTD.

Photo by J. Stephen Hall © Peter B. Kaplan 1986

TOP *Angela Lansbury introduces a performer at the concert.* **ABOVE** *Willie Nelson sings at the closing ceremonies.*

Photo by Eric Cohen © Peter B. Kaplan 1986

An earring made from a commemorative stamp, and its French counterpart. Based on a Peter B. Kaplan photograph, the stamps were issued by the U.S. and France on July 4, 1986. **RIGHT** *Closing ceremonies at Giant Stadium on July 6th included a 500-member marching band.*

Acknowledgements

With grateful appreciation to my publisher Fred Miller, whose encouragement, guidance and support has enabled me to fulfill a long-time dream of sharing my love for the Statue with the world.

And to countless others who have helped along the way, especially Michael Adlerstein, Karl Anderson, Pam Battaglin, Al Cerillo, Paul Chesley, Felice Kudman Ciccione, Monica Cipnic, Diane Dayson, Peter Dessauer, Ralph Dorazio, Bob Dotson, Milton Einbinder, Sidney Epstein, Joe Felice, Marty Forscher, Brian Feeney, Rick Globus, Harold Gordon, Michael Greene, Annie Griffiths, Butch Grucci, Ken Hansen, Joel Hecker, Jim & Brad Hill, Paul Hollerbach, Rene Hughes, James Irving, Alan Kalin, Gary Kelley, John Kidd, Robert Kraus, Robert Landsman, Kenneth Lassiter, Phil Lax, Norman Liss, Shawn Lowe, Jet Lowe, Jeffrey Marrazzo, Frank Mills, Phyllis Montgomery, Michael Newler, Tony & Harry O'Callaghan, Bill Pekala, Al Politi, Dominick Propati, Michael Radigan, Marianne Samenko, Carolyn Schafer, Marta Serra-Jovenich, Caroline Sheen, Lindsey Silverman, Victor Strauss, Manny Strumpf, Steve Tatti, Jimbo Thompson, Ellis Vener, Steve Weingrad, Richard Wells, David Wills, George Zambelli, and Peg Zitko.

To the many groups whose assistance allowed me to capture the Statue in her many moods and under all types of conditions: Allied Van Lines, Barrett Colea Inc., Ben Strauss, Inc., Bogen, Calumet, Captain and Crew of the Sally Ann, Eastman Kodak Professional Division, Globus Brothers Studio, Goodyear Airship Operations, Grossman Steel & Aluminum, Grucci Fireworks, Howard Brandston Lighting Designs, Linhof, Louis A. Nelson Inc., Marine Services, National Park Service, Nikon Professional Service, P.A. Fiebiger, Polaroid, Professional Camera Repair, Ruggieri Fireworks, Statue of Liberty-Ellis Island Foundation, Swanke Hayden Connell Architects, the US Coast Guard, and to the hundreds of men and women who were a part of this historic restoration.

And to those who are no longer with us, but for whose support over the years, I am forever grateful: Declan Haun, John Koeneman, Joan Hill, Bill Stetner, Tommy Walker and Bruno P. Zender.

Peter B. Kaplan